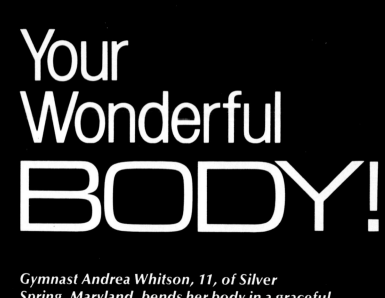

Your Wonderful BODY!

Gymnast Andrea Whitson, 11, of Silver Spring, Maryland, bends her body in a graceful arch. Her muscles, bones, heart, and lungs work together as a team to make this movement possible.

NATIONAL GEOGRAPHIC PHOTOGRAPHER JOSEPH H. BAILEY

COVER: Keeping fit. Darrick Day, 15, left, and Edward Mosher, 14, run for fun at a high school near their homes. Both boys live in Arlington, Virginia. Exercise, such as running, helps keep your body functioning at its best.

COTTON COULSON

BOOKS FOR WORLD EXPLORERS
NATIONAL GEOGRAPHIC SOCIETY

CONTENTS

If you could shrink to any size you wanted, you could explore inside the human body. The Bod Squad (right) does just that! You'll join these tiny cartoon characters in the pages of this book. Here, climbing into the throat, they begin their expedition into the body. Follow them as they continue on their journey.

"Why do I dream? How do I see? What is my blood made of?" You've probably asked yourself these questions and others like them. To prepare this book, we visited schools and talked with many groups of youngsters ages 8 through 13 to learn what they wanted to know about their bodies. Here, you'll find the answers to the questions they asked most often.

Copyright © 1982 National Geographic Society
Library of Congress CIP data: p. 104

JOYCE HURWITZ/ROZ SCHANZER

GO FOR IT!
bodies in action

The human body—your body—is often called a wonderful machine. It can perform remarkable feats of strength, muscle control, imagination, and reasoning. On these pages, you'll meet youngsters who have used brain and muscle to do outstanding things. In the chapters that follow, you'll read about the amazing body machinery that makes achievements like theirs possible. These youngsters have learned how to use their bodies to become winners. Perhaps you can, too!

Superstar swimmer Matthew Cerizo, of Wailuku, Hawaii, shows off some of the many medals he has won (right). Matthew, 14, holds 14 Hawaiian swimming records. His coach believes Matthew will someday break the world record in the 100-meter butterfly, his best event. Above, Matthew demonstrates his record-setting racing style. "When I compete, I think first of the time I want to make. Then I just concentrate on it," he says. "Winning takes practice and the mental power to stick with it."

4

It takes most people days to solve Rubik's Cube. Michael Mandell, 15 (right), can unscramble it in just 34 seconds! The challenge is to rotate the 54 colored squares so that each side of the cube becomes one solid color. That may sound easy, but there are more than 43 <u>quintillion</u> possible positions—and only one solution. "You need logical thinking and quick fingers," says Michael, who lives in Oak Park, Michigan. His secret? "I first work the top and bottom at the same time. Then I do the middle."

"The hardest part was getting the idea," says Patricia Powers about her award-winning poster (below). It took first place in the 1981 National Food Safety Poster Contest for fourth, fifth, and sixth graders. The award is presented by the U. S. Department of Agriculture. "I had to do several rough sketches," she says. Patricia, 12, lives in Cinnaminson, New Jersey. She hopes eventually to write and illustrate children's books. "It takes a lot of work to make a picture just right," she says. "Your imagination, your eyes, and your hands all have to work together perfectly."

MARTIN ROGERS

BOB KRIST

5

Reaching for the stars. At 13, Laura Jacobson is the youngest assistant and guide at the Eisenhower Observatory, in Hoffman Estates, Illinois. Below, she shows visitors the mirror of a telescope. Laura, who plans to become an astronomer, built her own telescope at home. "Now I want to build an observatory dome in my attic," she says.

Machelle Sweeting, 11, of New York City (below), was born with a hip defect. Doctors said she would never walk. But she was determined to walk, and started to exercise. Eventually, she began to run. Here, she races in the 1981 Colgate Women's games. She came in fourth out of 900 in her age group. "You have to believe in yourself," she says. "Never give up!"

LOWELL GEORGIA

Members of the Skip-Its jump-rope team practice double-Dutch jumping (above). It's one of 800 routines the Boulder, Colorado, team has learned. Elizabeth Bosely and Niel Aweida, both 14, turn the ropes. Derek Kuykendall and Kara Desmarais, both 10, jump. "Trick skipping takes coordination," Kara says. The 170-member team performs nationwide to raise money for heart research.

ROBERT M. LIGHTFOOT III

PAUL J. SUTTON/DUOMO

MARTHA COOPER

Young scientists Yaroslav Shoikhet, left, of New York City, and Michael Masterov, of Tenafly, New Jersey, demonstrate their prizewinning project (right). The boys, both 14, designed and built a miniature power plant that converts a certain kind of gas into electricity. "Our model is much more efficient than existing generating systems," says Yaroslav. "Even better, it doesn't pollute." To build the machine, the boys used parts collected in junk shops. It includes a computer control panel with 43 buttons and switches. "It took us eight months of constant redesigning to make the model work efficiently," says Yaroslav. The boys' project took first prize in four major science competitions.

Champion skater Corie Corrie, of Greenacres City, Florida, makes tough moves look easy. In 1981, Corie won a national championship. "To be a top skater, you have to practice, practice, practice!" she says. Corie, 10, practices 20 hours a week perfecting difficult spins and jumps. What does she like best about skating? "The excitement of winning," she says. Now that you've seen some things the human body can do, read on to find out about the amazing systems that make it all possible.

JOHN J. LOPINOT

1

ready, set,
GROW

Similar features link three generations. Susanna French, 8, of Bedford, New York, looks very much like her mother and her grandmother. Genes, parts of Susanna's cells, determined the color of her hair and eyes, as well as her other traits. She inherited exactly half of her genes from her mother, who inherited half from *her* mother. Below, twin Bod Squad members wave goodbye to each other on a dividing cell. As your body grows, each cell divides again and again.

JOYCE HURWITZ/ROZ SCHANZER

You began life as a single cell smaller than a pencil dot. That cell divided again and again —from one cell to two, two to four, four to eight, and so on. This began a process of cell reproduction that will continue for the rest of your life.

What are cells?

You've probably heard cells referred to as the building blocks of the body. Just as some houses are built of bricks, your body is built of cells. They are the basic units of life. Every part of your body consists of cells.

Cells differ in size, shape, and function. Still, most cells have certain things in common. The drawing on the next page shows some of the parts that most cells have and describes what they do.

Similar cells working together form tissue, such as muscle tissue. Various kinds of tissue working together form an organ, such as the stomach. One or more organs combined with other kinds of tissue form a system. A system performs a major function. The respiratory system, for example, takes in oxygen and sends it to all your cells.

What do my cells do?

Your trillions of cells work together to make you an active, thinking, feeling human being. They do the basic jobs that make all your systems work smoothly. Nerve cells carry messages throughout your body. Muscle cells contract, or tighten, and then relax so you can move. Skin cells help keep

Picture of health. Made by a computer, this picture shows that a baby girl is growing as she should. Together, the lines show high and low areas of the body. Doctors use such pictures to check the body's development during growth.

out harmful germs. White blood cells battle germs that get through. Red blood cells carry oxygen to all parts of your body. Bone cells increase the size of your skeleton to support your body as you grow.

How do cells work?

To do their basic job, most cells carry out hundreds of other individual tasks. Specialized bodies in each cell perform these tasks. These bodies, as a group, are called organelles. One organelle, the cell membrane, forms the cell wall. It admits nourishment into the cell and releases waste matter. Some organelles generate energy for the cell; others store the excess energy. One kind of organelle produces protein, the body's building material. Other organelles carry protein to the cell membrane for export to other parts of the body.

A cell's control center, called the nucleus, directs all the cell's activities. In the nucleus, structures known as chromosomes hold the plans for everything the cell does. Chromosomes use chemicals known as enzymes to signal the organelles to start or to stop their work.

One of a cell's most important jobs is making you grow. Cells do this by reproducing themselves. Each cell divides into two exact copies of the original, including chromosomes and all. As you read the previous paragraph, millions of your cells died. But they were all replaced through cell division. At the same time, your body produced enough extra cells to cause you to grow just a little.

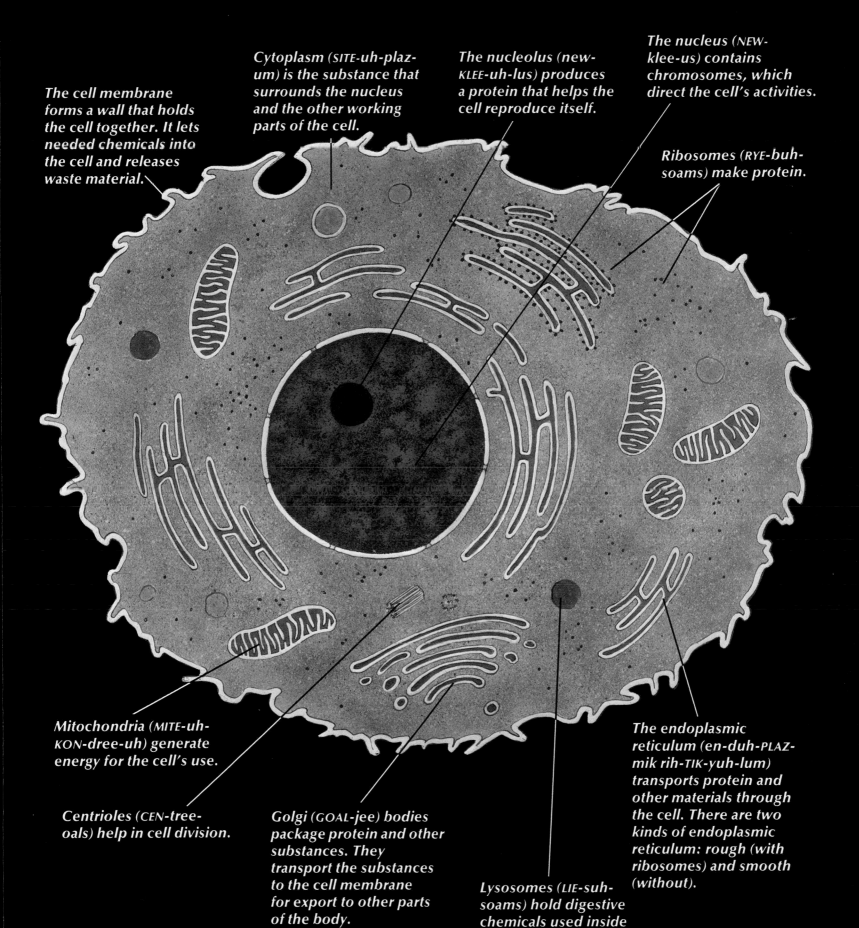

The cell membrane forms a wall that holds the cell together. It lets needed chemicals into the cell and releases waste material.

Cytoplasm (SITE-uh-plaz-um) is the substance that surrounds the nucleus and the other working parts of the cell.

The nucleolus (new-KLEE-uh-lus) produces a protein that helps the cell reproduce itself.

The nucleus (NEW-klee-us) contains chromosomes, which direct the cell's activities.

Ribosomes (RYE-buh-soams) make protein.

Mitochondria (MITE-uh-KON-dree-uh) generate energy for the cell's use.

Centrioles (CEN-tree-oals) help in cell division.

Golgi (GOAL-jee) bodies package protein and other substances. They transport the substances to the cell membrane for export to other parts of the body.

Lysosomes (LIE-suh-soams) hold digestive chemicals used inside

The endoplasmic reticulum (en-duh-PLAZ-mik rih-TIK-yuh-lum) transports protein and other materials through the cell. There are two kinds of endoplasmic reticulum: rough (with ribosomes) and smooth (without).

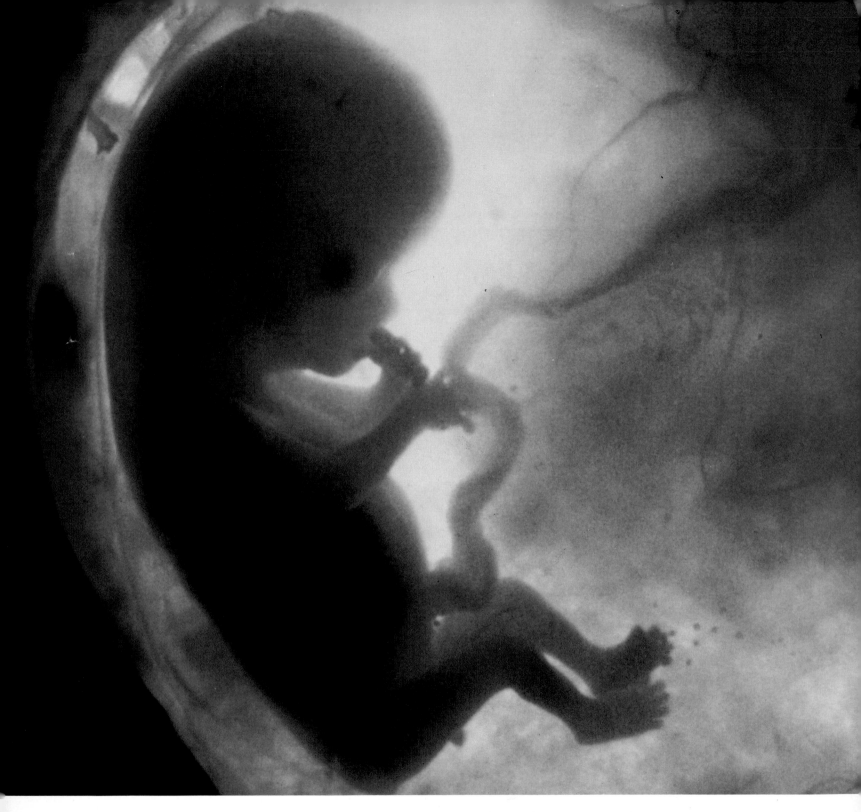

When do I grow the fastest?

You've already passed through your fastest stage of growth. It took place before you were born. The single cell from which you grew was a fertilized egg. During your first few weeks of life, that cell multiplied into billions of cells.

At first, all the cells were exactly alike, but they soon took on different shapes, sizes, and functions. The 46 chromosomes in the fertilized egg carried the plans for the production of all your different kinds of cells. Blood, nerve, muscle, and fat cells formed before you were born. By the time you were born, you had more than 200 different kinds of cells. Each kind had—and still has—its own job to do.

In the first months after birth, you grew rapidly. By the

COURTESY OF THE MARTIN S. CONNOR FAMILY

Some features change and others stay the same as a boy turns into a man. At 4, Jimmy Connor,

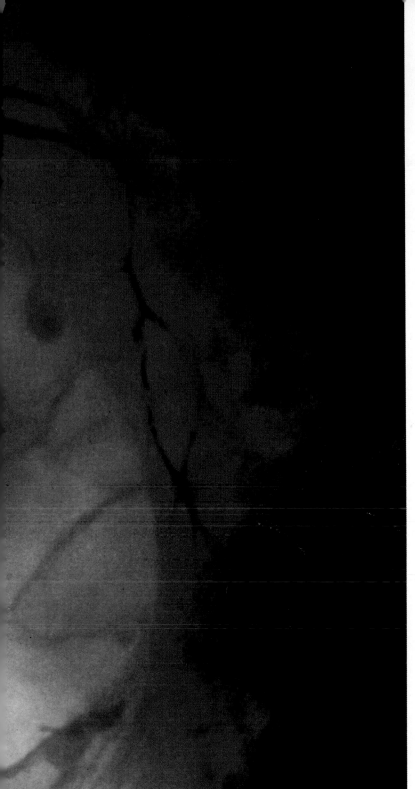

CECIL B. JACOBSON, M.D.

of Washington, D. C., has the round face and small features of early childhood (above, left). At 8, he has lost much of his baby fat (above). At 13, Jimmy has begun to look like an adult (left). His nose and his chin continue to grow. He now wears glasses, but the shape of his eyes remains the same —as do his dimples.

The fastest growth occurs in the first weeks of life (left). One fertilized egg cell divides over and over until it becomes a complete human being. This 16-week-old fetus (FEET-us), or unborn baby, measures 6 inches long (15 cm). Its major body parts are already formed. The fetus lives in a liquid-filled sac in the mother's uterus (YUTE-uh-rus). A tube called the umbilical cord carries nourishment from the mother's blood to the fetus. The cord is attached to the fetus's belly at a spot called the navel, or belly button.*

time you were a year old, you had grown half again as tall as you were at birth. Your weight had tripled. During childhood, you continue to grow, but more slowly. A final spurt of growth occurs during a special period called adolescence.

All people pass through the same stage of growth, but the stages come at different times for different people. You grow at your own pace—a pace different from those of your friends.

What's special about adolescence?

You enter adolescence as a child—you leave it as a young adult. During adolescence, not only do you grow larger, but other important changes take place as well.

Metric figures in this book have been rounded off.

13

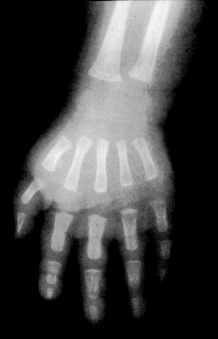

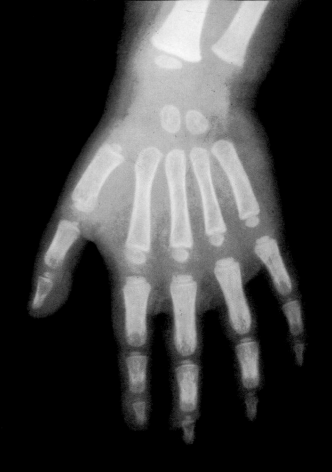

Stages in a person's growth show up in X rays of the hand and wrist. In the X rays on these pages, bone appears bright white. Skin and muscle tissue show paler white. In an infant's hand and wrist (above), only the larger bones have formed. Other bones are still cartilage— tough tissue that will later be replaced by bone. X rays like this one show doctors how much growing you still have to do. That's something a doctor can't always tell from your age alone.

By the time a child is 2, several small bones in the wrist have formed. The larger bones have continued developing and have grown.

Girls usually enter adolescence at an age be- tween 10 and 13. During adolescence, a girl's breasts develop and her hips widen. She grows body hair, and her reproductive organs mature.

Boys usually begin adolescence about a year lat- er than girls do. A boy's voice becomes deeper. His shoulders and chest broaden. Whiskers start sprouting from his face, and other body hair appears. His reproductive organs mature.

Physical changes aren't the only ones that occur during adolescence. You go through emotional changes, too. Part of you wants to stay a child, and part of you is eager to become an adult. You may find it hard to decide whether to stay home reading a book or to go out on a date. Your taste in music and in friends may do several flip-flops. Adoles- cence can be a confusing time!

Why do I look like my parents?

If people say you have your mother's eyes or your father's nose, it's not surprising. Your physical and mental characteristics depend on the master plan carried by your chromosomes. Half your chromo- somes came from your father, and half came from your mother. So you probably inherited some features from each parent.

The master plan carried by your chromosomes

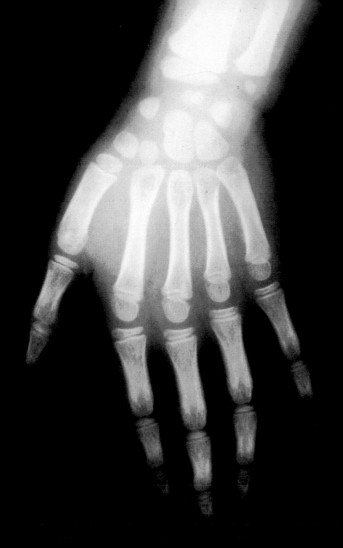

In the hand and wrist of this 6-year-old, 28 bones have formed. Another child of the same age might have fewer or more bones, depending on that child's growth rate.

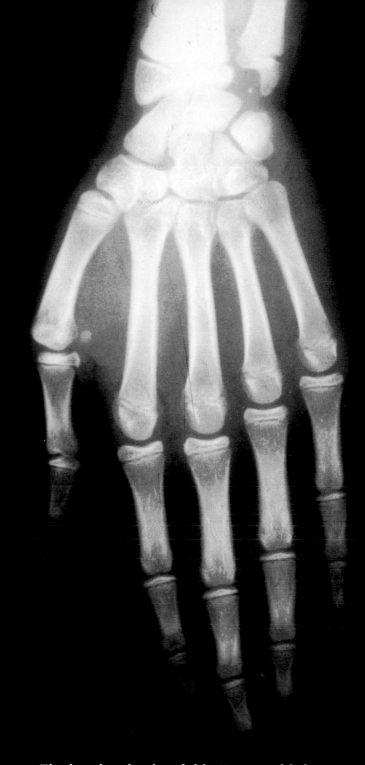

The hand and wrist of this 12-year-old show that the child is nearing adulthood. Nearly all the 30 bones in the hand and wrist are present. They are almost adult size.

consists of thousands of chemical particles called genes. Genes work in pairs—with one gene from your mother, and the other from your father. Each pair of genes has a specific job. Genes, in pairs and in groups of pairs, determine your traits—things such as hair color and the size of your earlobes. Genes are the keys to each part of your development.

Sometimes both genes in a pair are similar and work together to produce a particular feature. For example, if you inherited two genes for blond hair, you will have blond hair. Sometimes a pair of genes carry opposing instructions—let's say one gene for brown eyes, the other for blue eyes. In such cases,

Twins Patty and Barbie Torrento, 11, of San Francisco, California, share winning smiles. Identical twins result when a single fertilized egg divides into two duplicate eggs.

one gene will overpower the other and determine the feature by itself. A gene for brown eyes always overpowers a gene for blue eyes and produces brown eyes. The stronger gene is called a dominant gene. The weaker gene is called a recessive gene.

Each pair of genes you inherit can result in one of three possible combinations: recessive–recessive, recessive–dominant, dominant–dominant. Those three combinations, when they are multiplied by the tens of thousands of genes you possess, result in an almost unlimited variety of features you can inherit.

Some of your pairs of genes probably produced combinations that gave you the same features as one or both of your parents. Other combinations may have given you features similar to those of a brother or a sister, or of a more distant relative. The other millions of chance combinations, however, have given you your own unique look—unless you happen to be an identical twin.

What causes twins?

Identical twins develop from a single fertilized egg that splits into two identical eggs. The eggs then go on to develop normally into two separate people. Since they have the same genes, identical twins look exactly alike.

Twins can also grow from two separately fertilized eggs. The egg cells are different from each other. Each egg contains its own arrangement of chromosomes and its own

16

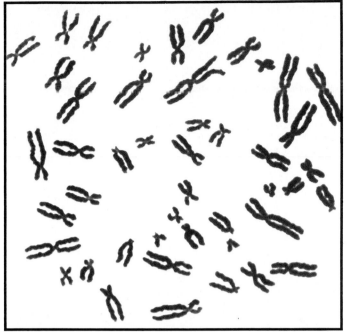

Chromosomes hold the master plan for all your physical and mental traits. The single cell from which you developed carried 23 pairs of chromosomes. That's 46 chromosomes in all. One chromosome in each pair came from your mother; the other chromosome came from your father. As the cell divided, the chromosomes reproduced themselves perfectly. Chromosomes carry thousands of units called genes. Genes determine specific traits—whether you will have freckles on the tip of your nose, for example. Genes work in pairs and in groups of pairs. Each parent contributed one gene of each pair. When genes in a pair are alike, they work together. When they are not alike, one gene overpowers the other. The particular combinations of genes you inherit determine how you will resemble—or not resemble —your parents and your other relatives.

All in the family. Brothers Steve Wallace, 12, left, and John, 10, of Carnation, Washington, closely resemble their father and their grandfather. Children are never exact copies of a parent, however, because each child inherits genes from each parent. The chromosomes that carry the genes can arrange themselves in any one of 8 million ways. The odds are strongly against your inheriting the same arrangement of chromosomes as a brother or sister who is not an identical twin. Mathematically, it works out to one chance in 70 trillion.

selection of genes. Twins produced from two different original egg cells are called fraternal twins. They look no more alike than any other brothers or sisters. One birth in 150 results in fraternal twins. One in 256 results in identical twins.

You may have wondered if there could be someone in the world, not related to you, who looks like you in every detail. Could that be possible? The chances are pretty slim. The odds against your having an exact look-alike form a number so large that it would fill 150 lines like the ones above!

17

Way to grow! Ralph Sampson, who plays center for the University of Virginia Cavaliers, towers over most people (right). He is 7 feet 4 inches tall (224 cm). Greg Manning, a guard for the Maryland Terrapins, stands 6 feet 1 inch (185 cm). In the United States, the average height for men is 5 feet 9 inches (175 cm). For women, it's 5 feet 4 inches (163 cm).

Growing Japanese. Since World War II, the height of the average Japanese has increased by 4 inches (10 cm). The reason? Changes in diet and customs. In this family the boy's father stands nearly a full head taller than his grandfather. The mother, too, is taller than the grandmother. Before World War II, the Japanese diet consisted mostly of rice, which lacks many nutrients. Since the war, the Japanese have begun eating a more varied diet, increasing their intake of protein and other nutrients. Also, Japanese used to sit kneeling on their lower legs, as the grandmother is doing. This posture hindered bone growth. Now most Japanese have adopted the Western custom of sitting on chairs.

Why do people stop growing at a certain age?

At the base of the brain rests a gland called the pituitary (pih-TOO-uh-tair-ee). Your genes largely determine how tall you can grow. But the pituitary primarily determines how fast you will grow and when you will stop growing.

The pituitary does this job through chemicals called hormones. Cells in the pituitary produce hormones. Carried by the bloodstream, hormones serve as STOP and GO signals for cell production. Periods of heavy hormone production result in growth spurts. About the time you reach 16 (if you're a girl) or 18 (if you're a boy), the pituitary signals ENOUGH! It reduces its output of hormones. Your body replaces worn-out cells, but it does not make any extra ones. As a result, you stop growing.

Is there anything I can do to make myself grow bigger?

You can help your body reach its maximum possible height in several ways. By eating the right foods, for example, you give your cells the fuel and the other raw materials they need to work at their best. Exercise also helps you grow. It builds your muscles and strengthens your heart. Rest is important, too. By getting enough rest, you give your cells a chance to slow down in their work and take care of any necessary repairs, such as mending a skinned knee. Many kinds of tissues grow their fastest as you sleep.

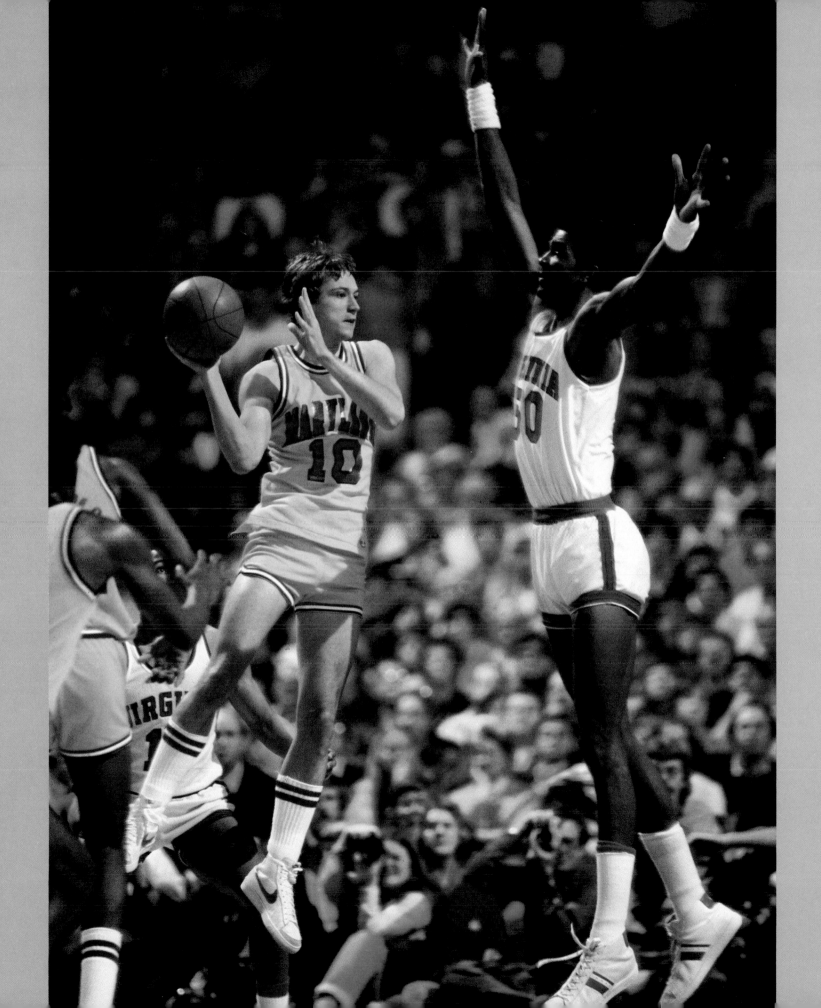

2

the
BRAIN:
your control center

It takes brain power to play a game of chess. Shabba Reid, 10, left, and Mark Arden, 12, both of Washington, D. C., study the board, plan strategy, and move their chessmen. Each player's thoughts and actions begin in the brain. It sends messages to the body along pathways of nerve cells. Below, members of the Bod Squad relay a message from the brain across a nerve cell to a muscle. The message tells the muscle to contract, causing movement.

JOYCE HURWITZ/ROZ SCHANZER

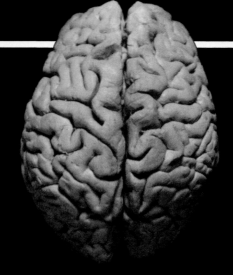

I f you had to choose one word to describe your brain, that word might be "busy!" Your brain works 24 hours a day to keep your body running smoothly. It is constantly making decisions. Every day, your brain analyzes and coordinates billions of bits of information gathered by your eyes, ears, and other sense organs.

In a very real way, your brain *is* you. The things you do that make you human—the person you are—begin in your brain. You may laugh when you're happy and cry when you're sad. You remember things that happened years ago. You play fast-paced games, solve complicated problems, and paint colorful pictures. Your imagination dreams up creatures that never existed and events that never happened. You understand things that your senses cannot detect—radio waves, for example. You can do all these things because the human brain is the most complex thing in the known universe. A computer that could do everything your brain can do would fill millions of buildings the size of New York City's World Trade Center towers.

Billions of nerve and other kinds of cells make up the cerebrum (suh-REE-brum), the largest part of your brain. The cerebrum controls reasoning, memory, and imagination.

Does my brain control everything I do?

Your brain controls thinking and feeling. It also controls most of your muscle activity. It assigns the control of your reflexes to your spinal cord. For example, if you accidently touch a bumblebee, your spinal cord gives the order to jerk your hand away. Your brain and spinal cord govern your entire network of nerves, called the nervous system. Together, the brain and spinal cord are called the central nervous system.

How does my nervous system give orders?

Your nervous system is a communications network reaching every cell in your body. Messages to and from the central nervous system constantly pass through the network. The nervous system contains billions of nerve cells, called neurons. There are trillions upon trillions of possible routes from any one part of the network to another. It would take a person more than a hundred years just to write out the zeros in the number of routes!

To pass messages along this network, nerve cells send out tiny jolts of electrical and chemical energy. These jolts are called impulses. They travel from cell to cell along fibers that branch out from the cell bodies. Messages coming into the central nervous system contain information about what is happening inside and outside the body. Messages sent out from the central nervous system tell the body how to react.

When did I start learning?

You began learning the moment you were born—and maybe even before that. Your learning may have begun with language—perhaps with the words "It's a boy!" or "It's a girl!" Recent studies show that newborn babies respond to spoken language. An infant moves in rhythm to speech. The speech can be in any language—but it cannot be gibberish. An American baby responds to a tape of a person speaking Chinese. (Infants show a preference for the female voice.) If the sound changes to something that is not language, the baby quickly loses interest.

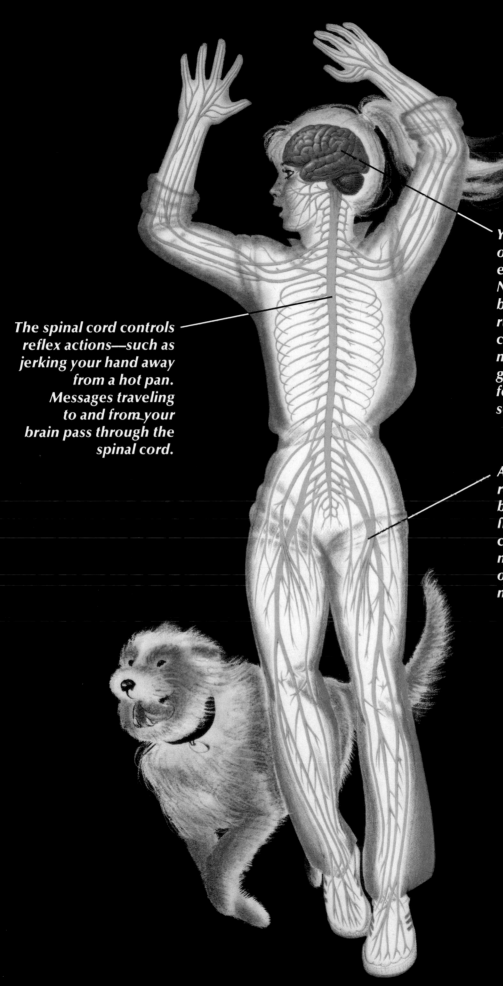

The spinal cord controls reflex actions—such as jerking your hand away from a hot pan. Messages traveling to and from your brain pass through the spinal cord.

Your brain is the center of everything you do and everything you are. Not only does your brain keep your body running smoothly and control most muscle movement, but it also governs your thinking, feelings, memory, and senses.

A network of nerves reaches every part of your body. Messages to and from the brain and spinal cord travel along this network. Nerves consist of many individual neurons, or nerve cells.

PHOEBE DUNN

Playing the violin brings millions of nerve cells into action (left). To make music, Molly Hanson, 9, of New Canaan, Connecticut, reads the score, moves the bow, hears the notes, and makes decisions on volume and tone. She calls on different control centers in her brain for each action.

The drawing at right shows some areas of the cerebrum that control mental and physical activities. Each area is constantly exchanging messages with other parts of the body. Even a simple movement —let's say swatting a fly—requires the exchange of thousands of messages in a split second.

Hands and eyes work together as Jeff Myers, 14, of Sacramento, California, draws a picture of the Queen Mary (below). As Jeff works, his brain coordinates the movement of his hands with his sight. As a result, the lines go on the paper where Jeff wants them to go.

TOM MYERS

How do I learn?

When you learn, nerve cells in your brain pass information back and forth in a complicated pattern no computer can match. Suppose you taste a pineapple for the first time. Your brain receives taste sensations from your mouth and smell sensations from your nose. In a flash, it compares the flavor with every other flavor you have experienced. It identifies the flavor as new. Then it stores the new sensation. At the same time, it identifies the look of the pineapple, as well as the sound of the word "pineapple." From now on, whenever you taste, smell, or see a pineapple, or hear the name, you can call up any of these stored experiences. You can identify the fruit immediately.

Learning takes place in the cerebrum (suh-REE-brum), the largest part of the brain. The cerebrum consists of two halves, called hemispheres. Usually, the left hemisphere controls reasoning ability—such as the ability to use language or to use math. The right hemisphere governs imagination and artistic ability. Some people tend to use one side of their cerebrum much more than the other. Such people are apt to be more logical than artistic—or vice versa.

24

BODY MOVEMENT

SPEECH

BODY SENSATION

SMELL

READING

MEMORY

HEARING

SIGHT

How much can I learn?

Scientists say that most people use less than their full brain-power during their lifetime. So you probably can learn much more than you might have thought possible. But people differ in what they learn best. You may, for example, find grammar difficult but be a whiz at math. A friend may learn to play the guitar with ease—but find history a real disaster. If you set your mind to it, though, you may well be able to learn just about anything you want to learn.

ROZ SCHANZER

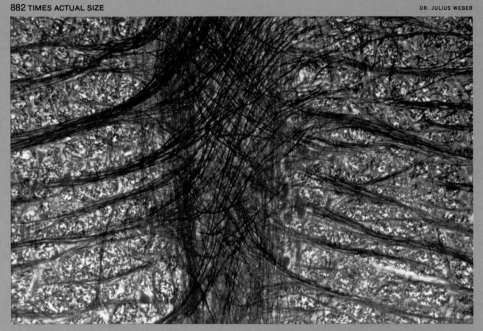

Rub your belly with your right hand, and pat your head with your left. Can you guess which side of your brain ordered each movement? . . . Guess again! The nerves that branch down from each side of the brain cross each other at the back of the head (above). As a result, the left side of your brain controls the right side of your body,

and vice versa. The two halves of your cerebrum share certain duties, such as control of arm movement. But when it comes to thought, each half has its own separate areas of responsibility. Usually, the left side deals with practical thought, such as numbers and language. Artistic thought begins in the right half.

Can I increase my brainpower?

Yes, you can—by keeping your mind as active as possible. Take up as many activities as you can manage. Try improving on a skill you may not be so good at. It may be painting or tennis or solving puzzles. The more experiences you bring to your brain, the more raw material it will have for thinking, analyzing, and creating.

Another way to increase your brainpower is to develop good study habits. Here's one tip: You'll concentrate better without distractions such as television. Your teacher can give you more hints for getting the most out of your study time.

How does my brain make my muscles work?

Like all the other parts of your body, your muscles receive messages from your brain. When you want to swing a tennis racket, the area of the cerebrum that controls arm and hand movement sends out thousands of signals in the form of electrical impulses. The impulses travel along nerve pathways from your brain to your arm

and hand. When the impulses reach your muscles, you swing the racket, just as you had planned.

The cerebrum orders muscles into action. Another part of the brain, the cerebellum (sehr-uh-BEL-um), coordinates the actions of different muscles into one smooth motion. It does this by checking on the message traffic between cerebrum and muscle cells. It makes sure all the messages flow in the right order. The cerebellum lies just below the back of the cerebrum.

The muscles that keep your heart pumping and your other organs functioning do their work without any thought on your part. Day and night, they do their jobs without your making a decision to put them to work. You might forget to eat your lunch one day. But when you do eat, you can't forget to digest your food. Signals that tell your internal organs to work come from the brainstem. That's a section of the brain below the cerebrum. People cannot normally control functions directed by the brainstem.

Crouched at the starting block, a runner waits to begin a race (above). In such voluntary activity as running, messages from the brain set the body in motion. The messages race down the runner's spinal cord to the nerves in his leg. The branching nerves carry the "Go!" messages to the muscles in his leg. In a split second, the runner will push off the starting block. As he runs, sensory nerves in his feet and legs will send progress reports to his brain.

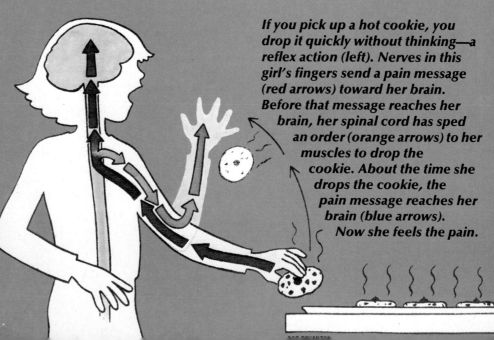

If you pick up a hot cookie, you drop it quickly without thinking—a reflex action (left). Nerves in this girl's fingers send a pain message (red arrows) toward her brain. Before that message reaches her brain, her spinal cord has sped an order (orange arrows) to her muscles to drop the cookie. About the time she drops the cookie, the pain message reaches her brain (blue arrows). Now she feels the pain.

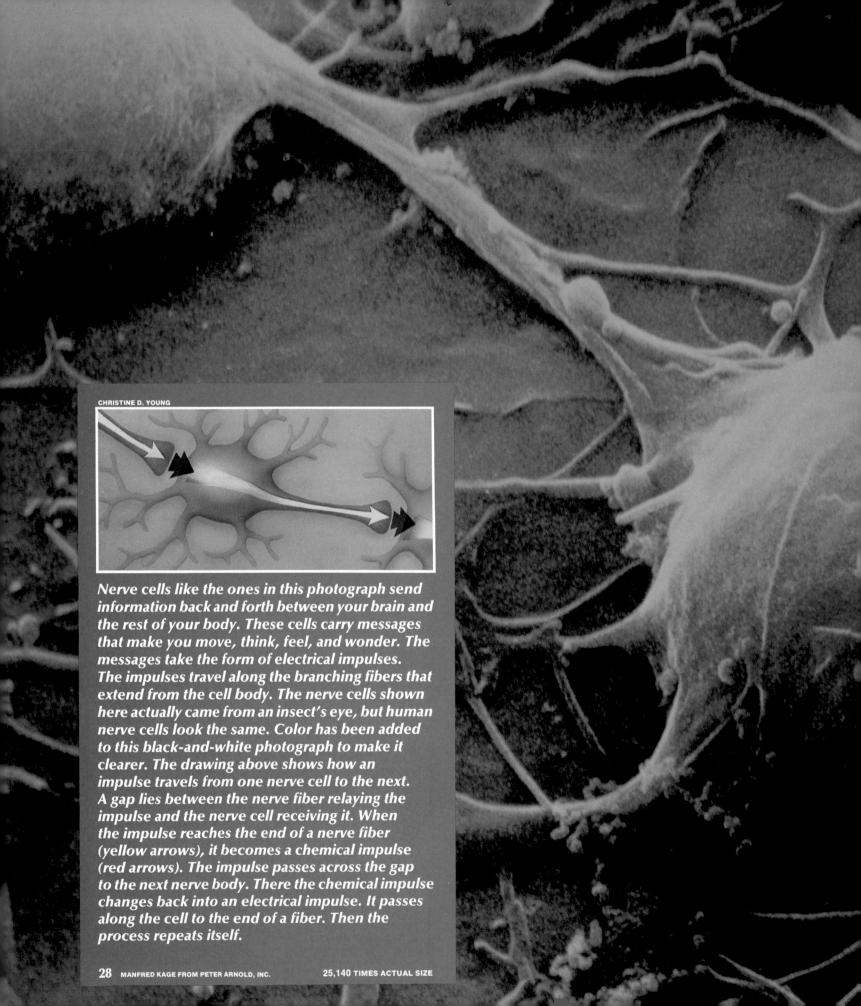

CHRISTINE D. YOUNG

Nerve cells like the ones in this photograph send information back and forth between your brain and the rest of your body. These cells carry messages that make you move, think, feel, and wonder. The messages take the form of electrical impulses. The impulses travel along the branching fibers that extend from the cell body. The nerve cells shown here actually came from an insect's eye, but human nerve cells look the same. Color has been added to this black-and-white photograph to make it clearer. The drawing above shows how an impulse travels from one nerve cell to the next. A gap lies between the nerve fiber relaying the impulse and the nerve cell receiving it. When the impulse reaches the end of a nerve fiber (yellow arrows), it becomes a chemical impulse (red arrows). The impulse passes across the gap to the next nerve body. There the chemical impulse changes back into an electrical impulse. It passes along the cell to the end of a fiber. Then the process repeats itself.

    25,140 TIMES ACTUAL SIZE

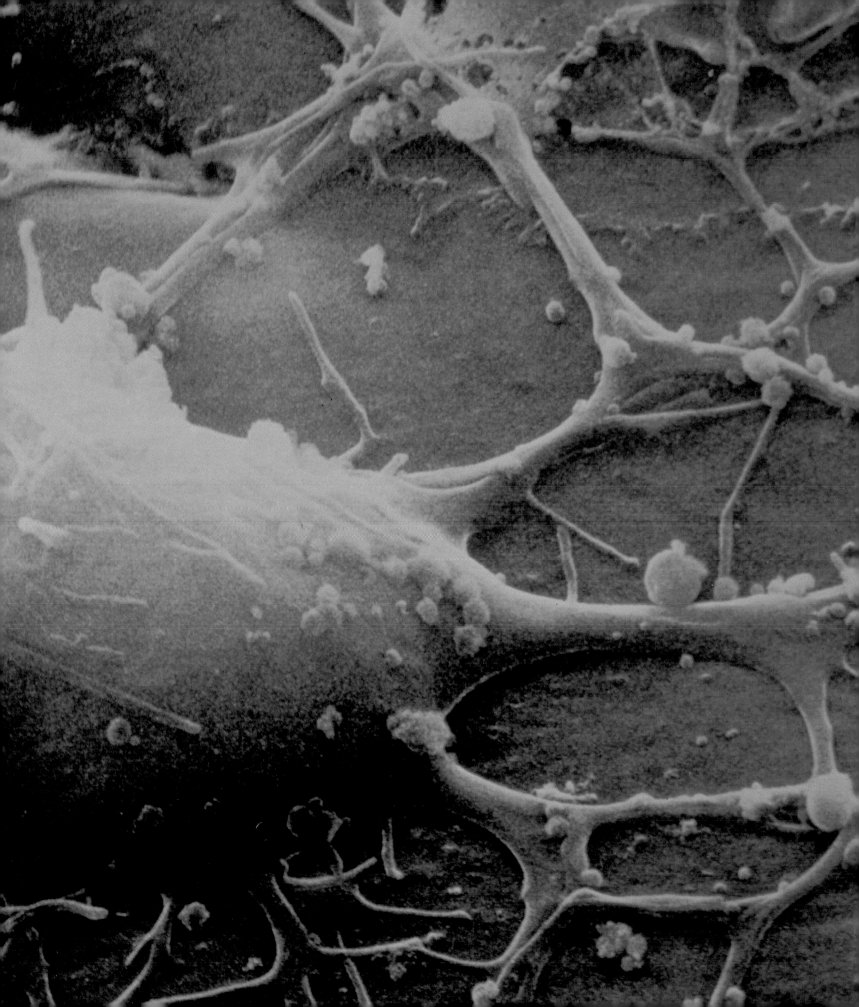

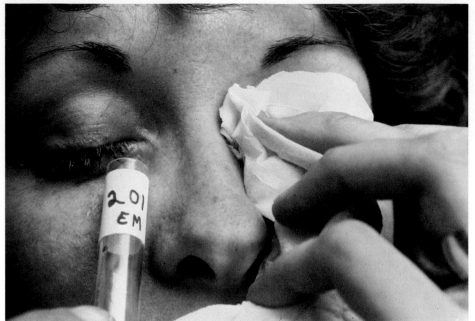

Tears collected in a test tube (left) help scientists study links between emotions and chemical changes in the body. In this study, volunteers collected their tears after they watched a sad movie and after they sniffed raw onions. Scientists analyzed both kinds of tears (below). The study showed that the chemical content of tears caused by emotions differs from that of tears caused by irritants. Emotional crying may rid your body of harmful chemicals that collect when you're feeling sad or angry.

Why do I have feelings?

Everyone feels a wide variety of emotions, such as love, anger, happiness, and fear. Although no one knows for sure, some scientists believe that early humans developed emotions as a way of making sure they filled their bodies' needs. If they kept themselves warm, well fed, and out of danger, their brains rewarded them with feelings of pleasure. When danger threatened, or when a need went unfilled, their brains alerted them with unpleasant feelings.

Your emotions arise in a deep part of the brain called the limbic system. You have little control over the emotions you feel, but a good deal of control over your response to emotions. If you suddenly come face to face with a bear in the woods, your limbic system will make you feel fear. You may feel like running. But your cerebrum, the part of the brain that thinks, tells you that you'll be safer if you stay motionless. You take control of your response to the fear. You stay still. The bear walks away.

Are happy people healthier than people who are sad or worried?

More and more, scientists are finding links between mental health and physical health. They have learned that strong emotions can affect certain bodily functions. People who overreact to pressure, for example, run a greater risk of heart disease than do people who take pressure in stride. It also works the other way around: People who take good care of their bodies are generally happier than people who neglect their sleep, exercise, and nutrition.

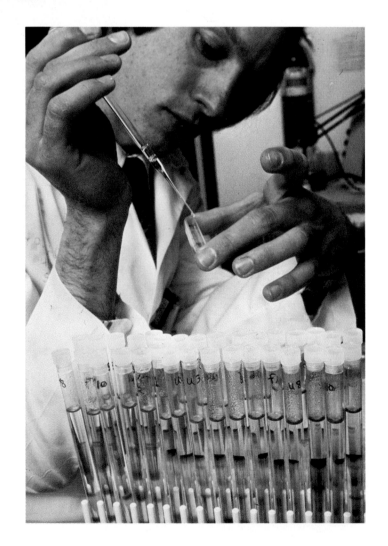

30

Many people feel love for a pet. Beth Givens, 12, of Sunnyvale, California, hugs her dog, Marilyn. All your emotions, from joy to rage, begin in your brain.

LIANE ENKELIS

What happens when I sleep?

During sleep, your body takes a rest. Your heart rate and your rate of breathing slow down. Your muscles relax. Part of your brain relaxes, too. The flow of information from your senses to your brain trails off. You don't hear the TV or people talking in another room. A loud noise, such as an alarm clock ringing, may wake you up, but most outside noises don't disturb you. With your body working at a slower pace, your brain occupies itself in one of its least understood activities: dreaming.

Why do I dream?

No one knows for certain why people dream. However, scientists are coming close to some answers. They study dreaming by checking the brain activity of people sleeping in a laboratory. They use an instrument that picks up the electrical impulses in the people's brains. It records the impulses as wavy lines (right, above). The lines tell the scientists the amount and kind of mental activity that is taking place.

During your waking hours, your brain works hard analyzing the millions of bits of information that flood into it. It links your thoughts in logical order so you can solve problems and learn new things.

During a dream, you enter a completely different world. Your mind wanders free. Have you ever tried to control a dream? You can't. Logic and conscious thought are strangers to the dream process.

In real life, you must obey rules. In a dream, there are no rules. Any kind of dream is possible. Some dreams are pleasant. Others are scary or upsetting. You've probably had some dreams that were downright *weird!* You might fly in a dream, or polka-dotted kangaroos might whistle. Dreams of all kinds are perfectly normal. Everybody has them.

Scientists have found that dreaming is good for you. It lets you experience feelings and situations that may make you uncomfortable in real life. In this way, dreaming lets you release emotional energy that has built up during your waking, conscious hours.

You do most of your dreaming during a stage of sleep called REM —for Rapid Eye Movement. During

REM sleep, your closed eyes move rapidly from side to side. Your dreams are especially vivid.

Scientists say that all dreams, from pleasant to scary to far-out, are normal. Dreaming gives you a chance to roam free from the rules of everyday life. It serves as a safety valve for your built-up emotions.

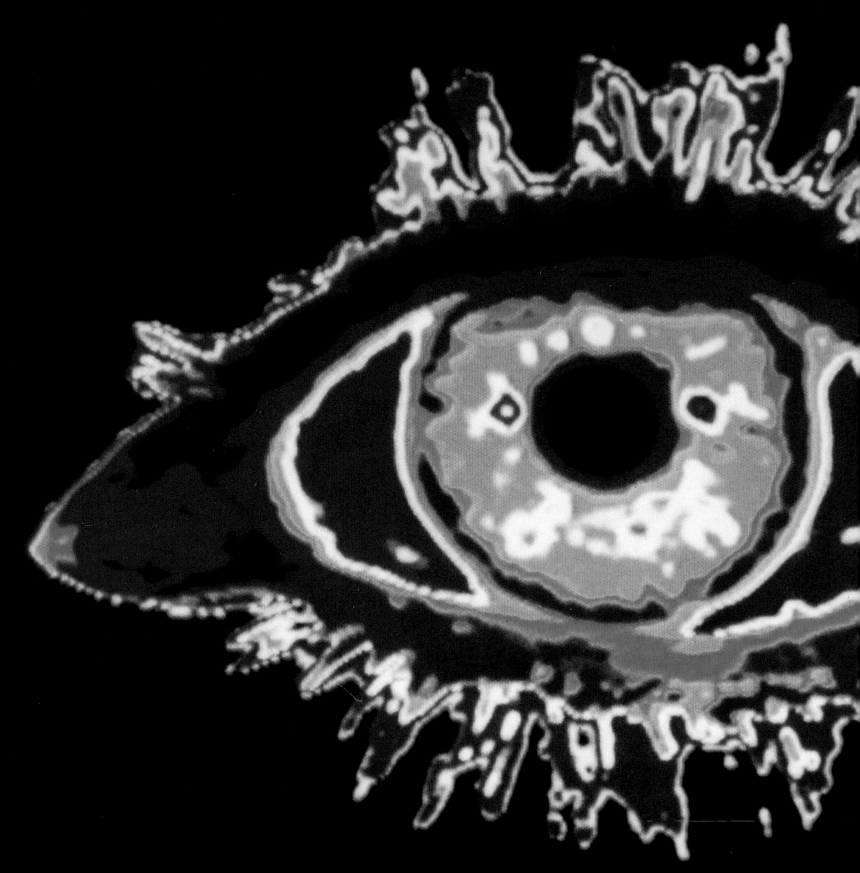

Almost everything you know came to you through your eyes. Your eyes help you recognize form, size, color, movement, *and distance. In this picture, made with a special camera, a computer has added color to make the parts of the eye clearly visible.*

HOWARD SOCHUREK

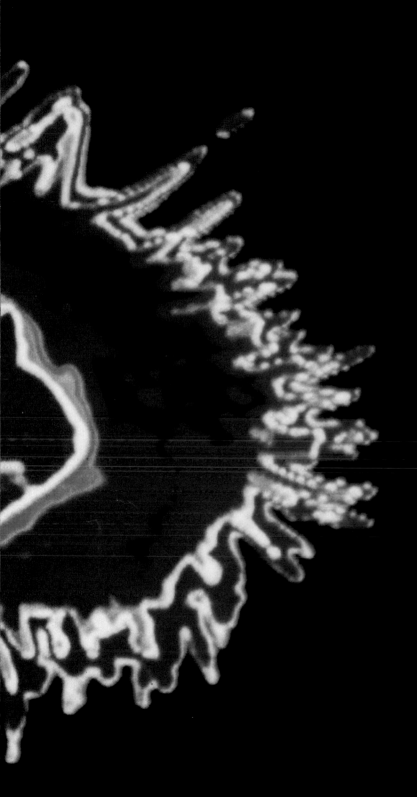

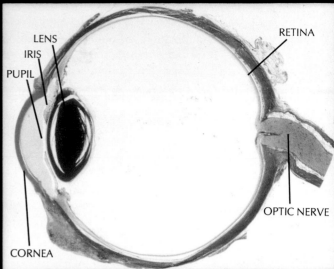

LENS
IRIS
PUPIL
RETINA
CORNEA
OPTIC NERVE

This side view of the eye shows its parts.
Sight is the sharpest of your senses.

How do I see?

Like your other sense organs, your eyes are almost constantly gathering information. Millions of light-sensitive nerve cells in the back of each eye relay the information to your brain through a bundle of nerve fibers that form the optic nerve. Your brain analyzes the information, and you see. The whole process takes only a fraction of a second.

Light enters your eye through the cornea (KOR-nee-uh), a transparent part of the eye's tough, outer layer. If you look in a mirror, you can see your eye's colored iris. It automatically controls the amount of light that enters your eye through an opening called the pupil. In bright light, muscles in the iris close your pupil to a pinpoint. This blocks out much of the light. In dim light, the pupil opens wide, letting in more light.

Behind the iris lies the lens. The lens focuses light onto the retina (RET-nuh), the back wall of your eye. To focus, the lens changes shape. It flattens out for distance vision and becomes rounder for near vision. In a single day, your lens may change shape 100,000 times.

There's more to the ear than meets the eye! Below, Bod Squad members show how hearing works. Sound waves enter the ear and strike the eardrum (A), causing it to vibrate. The vibrations continue through a series of three bones (B) extending from the eardrum. They pass to fluids inside the cochlea (KOK-lee-uh) (C). The vibrations stimulate nerve cells lining the cochlea. The cells send impulses to the brain along the auditory nerve (D). In a similar way, nerve cells in the semicircular canals (E) send balance signals to the brain.

JOYCE HURWITZ/ROZ SCHANZER

How do I hear?

A coyote howls at night, sending out vibrations called sound waves. It takes the sound waves about five seconds to reach you at your campsite a mile away (1 ½ km).

Your external ear—the part you can see—acts as a funnel to catch the vibrations and pass them on. The vibrations travel along a passageway called the auditory canal. Then they strike the eardrum, causing it to vibrate. Behind the eardrum, the vibrations pass through a series of three tiny bones. In the process, the strength of the vibrations triples.

The last bone vibrates against a spiral structure called the cochlea (KOK-lee-uh). Fluid inside the cochlea begins vibrating. As it does, it stimulates thousands of nerve cells that line the cochlea. These cells send impulses to the hearing center in your cerebrum. You hear the coyote's *"OWOOooooo"* —and you slide deeper into your sleeping bag!

The inner ear, where the cochlea is located, helps you keep your balance, as well as hear. Three fluid-filled loops, the semicircular canals, are attached to your cochlea. Nerve cells line the canals. One loop senses upward and downward motion. Another senses forward and backward motion. The third senses sideways motion.

Normally, the fluids are level. If you lose your balance, the fluids slosh around. The nerve cells flash a message to your brain that the fluids are not level. Your brain then signals other parts of your body to help you regain your balance.

The Apple Turnover, a popular ride at Kings Dominion amusement park outside Richmond, Virginia, whirls around 30 times a minute (above). After a $1^1/_2$-minute ride, a visitor to the park is so dizzy she hangs onto the handles as she gets out of the car (left). During the ride, fluids in her inner ear sloshed around. The fluids touch cells that send signals about balance to her brain. The ride caused the fluids to splash so violently that her brain received confused signals. As a result, she felt dizzy. You've probably experienced the same spinning sensation after a carnival ride. Now that the girl is back on solid ground, the fluids in her inner ear will return to level. Her sense of balance will return to normal.

MATTHEW NEAL McVAY

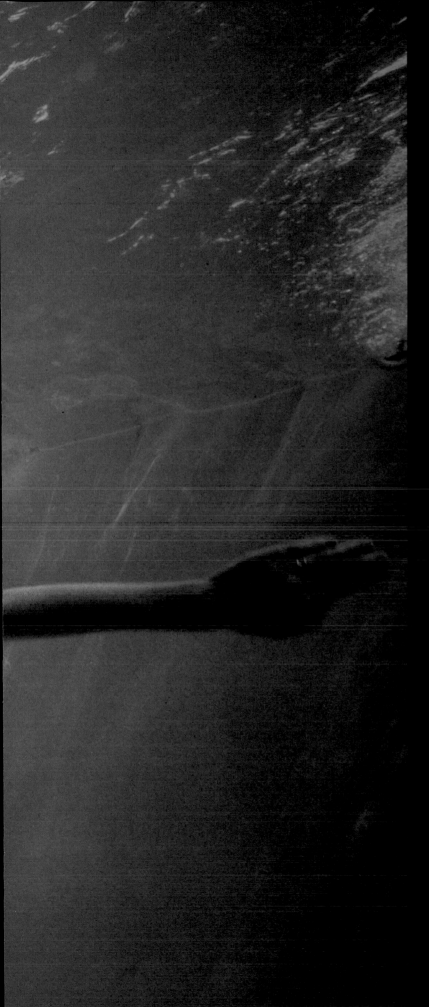

3

the
BREATH
of life

Swimming underwater, Cia Froelich, 13, in foreground, and Julia Griner, 14, both of New York, New York, hold deep breaths of air in their lungs. To carry out their jobs, your body's cells need a steady supply of oxygen. The cells get the oxygen from the air you breathe. The air travels down your windpipe to your lungs. Members of the Bod Squad (below) free-fall through the windpipe. They're on their way to the lungs to find out how oxygen from air reaches the cells.

JOYCE HURWITZ/ROZ SCHANZER

Just as a fire needs oxygen to burn, the cells of your body need oxygen to generate energy. Oxygen is a gas. It makes up one-fifth of the air you breathe.

Your respiratory system draws fresh air into your body and sends used air back out. In the lungs, oxygen from the incoming air passes into your bloodstream. Your bloodstream delivers the oxygen to every cell in your body.

At rest, you take about 14 breaths a minute. That's 20,000 a day. In a lifetime of 70 years, you will breathe 515 million times. You will take in 13½ million cubic feet of air (382,280 m³)—enough to fill 64 Goodyear blimps!

Is the air I inhale the same as the air I exhale?

No, it isn't. When you inhale, the air that enters your lungs contains oxygen. When you exhale, the air expelled from your lungs contains a gas called carbon dioxide. Your cells use oxygen for energy production. They leave carbon dioxide as waste. You get rid of the waste when you exhale.

Plants use the carbon dioxide you exhale to make food. The plants, in turn, release oxygen as a waste product. This exchange keeps the amount of oxygen and carbon dioxide in the air in balance. It helps keep plants, animals, and people going.

How do I breathe?

Your lungs have no muscles of their own. Instead, they rely on muscles in the chest cavity to cause the

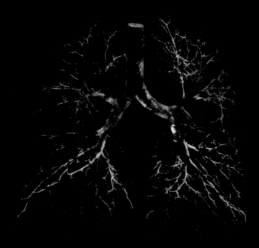

Inside your lungs, the bronchial (BRONG-kee-uhl) passages form a structure that looks like an upside-down tree. The bronchial tree divides into 30,000 tubes. The tubes carry air into and out of your lungs.

motions that make you breathe.

Inhaling results from muscle contraction. Exhaling results from muscle relaxation. The contraction of muscles in the chest cavity causes the cavity to become larger. That makes room for the lungs to expand. As the lungs expand, air pressure inside them drops. Air of higher pressure from the outside rushes in to equalize the pressure in the lungs. As a result, you inhale.

When the muscles relax, they spring back into position against the lungs. That squeezes air out, causing you to exhale.

Can I forget to breathe?

You can't forget to breathe, because you never have to remember to breathe. An area of your brain called the respiratory center makes sure that you keep breathing, even when you are asleep. It sends signals automatically to the muscles that cause breathing. It's a good thing you don't rely on memory to breathe. Brain cells can live for only about four minutes without oxygen.

Your respiratory center adjusts the speed and depth of your breathing. Suppose you run a foot race with a friend. To provide the energy you need, your muscle cells burn up oxygen more quickly than they do when you are walking. They release carbon dioxide rapidly into the bloodstream. By doing so, the cells signal the respiratory center that they need more oxygen. The respiratory center also receives messages from other kinds of cells, such as those in your joints. It responds immediately by making you breathe quickly and deeply.

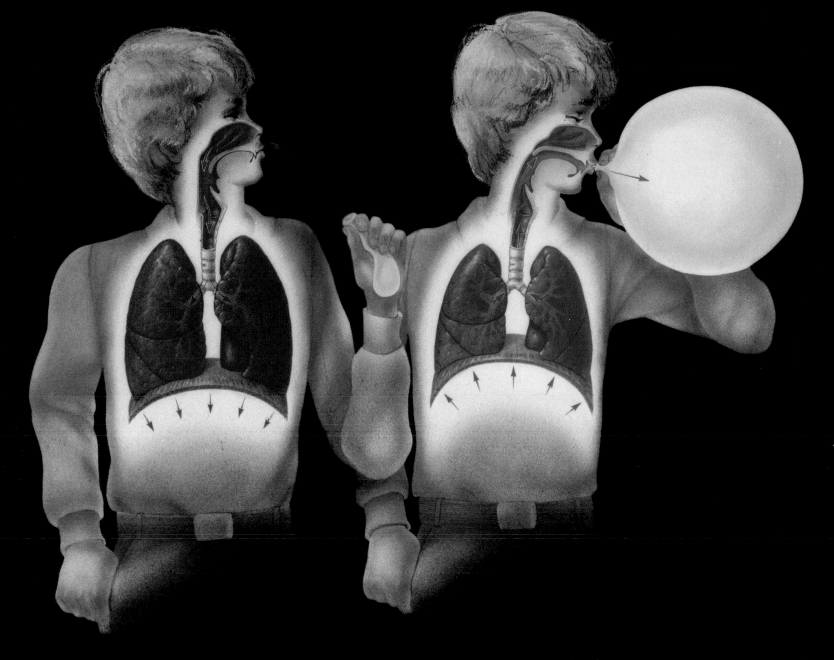

As this boy takes a deep breath to blow up a balloon, muscles in his chest spring into action. His diaphragm (DIE-uh-fram), a large muscle just below his lungs, flattens somewhat. Other muscles swing the ribs slightly outward. These actions reduce the air pressure inside his lungs. Air rushes in through his nose, filling the lungs and equalizing the pressure. When the boy's muscles relax, he exhales. His diaphragm springs back into its dome shape. His ribs close inward. The combined actions squeeze the lungs, forcing the air out.

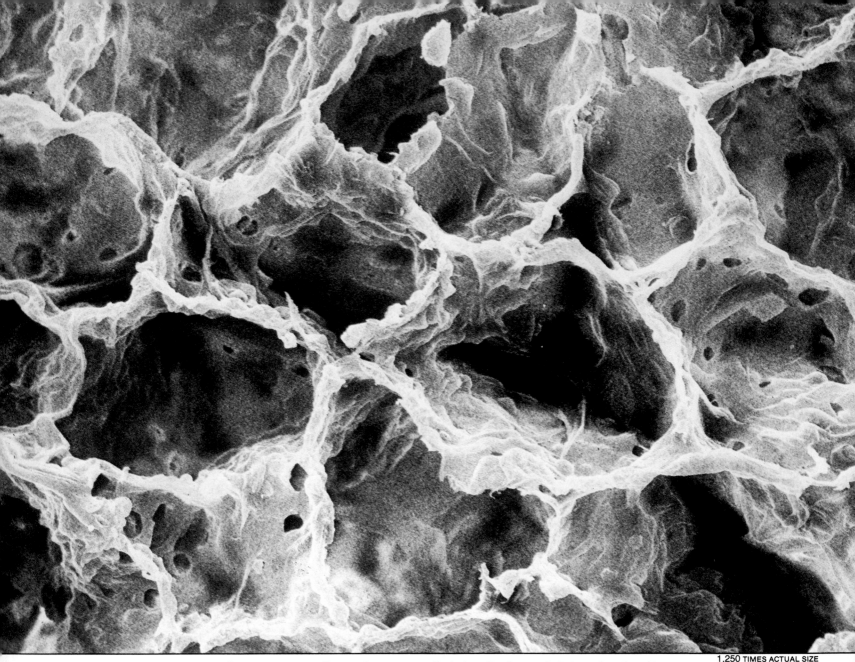

1,250 TIMES ACTUAL SIZE
MARILYN J. KOERING

Your lungs contain millions of air sacs, called alveoli (al-VEE-uh-lie). In the alveoli, your body exchanges carbon dioxide for oxygen.

How does oxygen get into my bloodstream?

On its way to the lungs, inhaled air whooshes through a series of smaller and smaller passages. It goes from the trachea (TRAY-kee-uh), or windpipe, into the two bronchi (BRONG-kie). The bronchi branch into smaller tubes called bronchioles. In turn, the bronchioles branch off, becoming smaller with each division. The smallest bronchioles carry air to the alveoli (al-VEE-uh-lie), parts of your lungs that pass oxygen to the blood.

Alveoli are tiny air sacs with walls only one cell thick. They cluster at the end of each bronchiole. An adult's lungs contain 300 million alveoli. If all these alveoli were spread out, they would cover a surface the size of a tennis court.

Tiny blood vessels called capillaries surround the alveoli. Once inside the alveoli, oxygen passes through the air sacs' thin walls. Then it passes through the walls of the capillaries and into the bloodstream. There, the oxygen attaches itself to red blood cells, which carry it to your body's other cells.

As oxygen moves into the blood, an exchange is actually taking place. Carbon dioxide that has been expelled by your cells passes out of the blood and into the alveoli. The carbon dioxide flows up through the bronchial tree and leaves the body in exhaled breath.

Inside a cluster of alveoli (right), air flows through tunnels to reach each individual air sac (arrow). The air contains oxygen. Atmospheric pressure —pressure created by the weight of the air around you—helps force the oxygen through the alveolar walls. This painting shows alveoli many hundreds of times their actual size. The painting below shows a section of alveolar wall. It is enlarged even more. The wall is only one cell thick. Beside the wall runs a network of tiny blood vessels called capillaries. Here, you see one capillary.

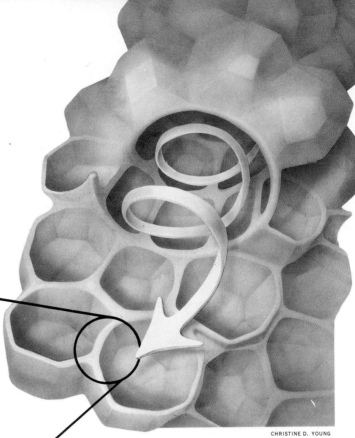

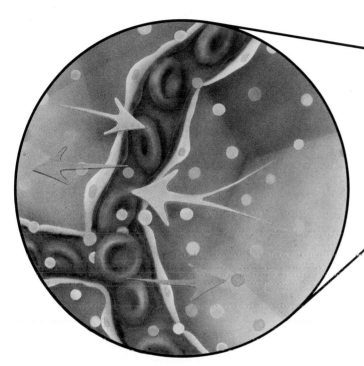

After oxygen molecules (blue circles, left) pass through the alveolar wall, they enter the capillaries. They attach themselves to red blood cells. The blood flows through the body, carrying a fresh supply of oxygen to the cells. As oxygen enters the bloodstream, the blood releases carbon dioxide (gold circles) through the alveolar wall. Carbon dioxide is a waste product released by the cells as they burn oxygen. The carbon dioxide leaves the body as you exhale.

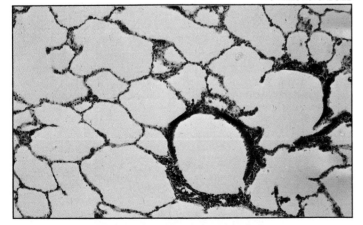

178 TIMES ACTUAL SIZE

173 TIMES ACTUAL SIZE

Healthy lung tissue looks like this (above). It has a pink, clean appearance. Tissue from a lung of a smoker is dark and dirty (above, right). Tar and other harmful substances in cigarette smoke discolor the

tissue. Worse, they damage or destroy the tissue. This makes the body work harder for the oxygen it needs. People who smoke increase their risk of getting lung cancer, emphysema, and heart disease.

43

How do I smell different smells?

You walk into your kitchen and smell cookies baking. At the beach, you smell the tangy scent of the sea. In a garden, the smell of roses fills the air. The cookies, the sea, and the roses all give off invisible clouds of molecules. The molecules of one substance are different from those of another. As you breathe, the molecules enter your nose and affect your olfactory system. That's the part of your body that gives you a sense of smell.

Let's say you smell bacon frying. When the bacon molecules enter your nose, they pass into the sticky mucus that lines the nasal passages. The molecules pass along the mucus to the olfactory membrane. That's a patch of tissue at the top of each nostril, right behind the bridge of your nose. This membrane is made of sensor cells that send messages about scents to your brain. You know that things smell stronger if you give them a good sniff. That's because sniffing carries the molecules up to your olfactory membrane in more force than ordinary breathing does.

Hairlike cell parts called cilia grow from the surface of the olfactory membrane. When the bacon molecules meet the cilia, they set off a chemical reaction. The reaction starts a signal traveling from the cilia along a network of nerves to the brain. The signal ends up in your cerebrum, which decodes it. The decoding results in your smelling the bacon.

You have probably noticed that certain scents remind you of people or events in your life. A perfume or a cooking aroma may remind you of your grandmother. The smell of pine trees may remind you of swapping ghost stories at night on a camp-out. Of all the senses, the sense of smell triggers the strongest memories. As the scent signal flashes from cilia to cerebrum, it passes through the limbic system. That is the part of your brain that governs memory and emotion. Scientists think this may be the reason that smells so often remind people of the past.

How many kinds of things can I smell?

Your nose is quite sensitive. You can detect up to 10,000 different scents. Just a few molecules of a substance, among millions of other molecules, are all you need to pick up the scent of that substance. Most animals have even sharper senses of smell. Some moths can detect the scent of another moth more than 2 miles away (3 km). To track down a criminal, a bloodhound follows the body scent that has passed to the ground through the criminal's shoes!

Without a sense of smell, you could not enjoy your food as much as you do. Your sense of taste can detect only four tastes: sweetness, sourness, bitterness, and saltiness. Your sense of smell adds more information. Read more about your senses of smell and taste, and how they work together, on page 56.

Prisca Weems, 12, of Washington, D. C., smells a rose. The drawing at right shows what happens as she draws in the fragrant air.

BILL WEEMS

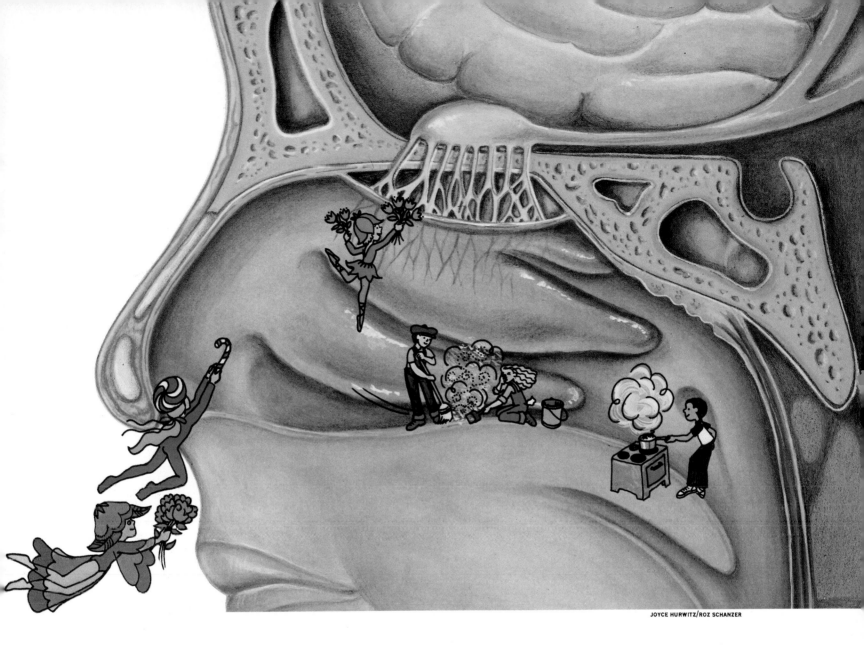

Several different things happen to the air you breathe as it passes through your nose. The Bod Squad, above, shows some of the jobs your nasal passages do. When you breathe air in, your nasal passages clean it, moisten it, and warm or cool it. Tiny hairs near the inside front of your nose trap dust particles. Mucus lines your inner nasal passages. The mucus catches particles that escape the hairs. In the mucus, tiny hairlike cell parts called cilia beat rhythmically back and forth. They sweep trapped particles toward the back of your throat. There the particles are harmlessly swallowed with your saliva. These defenses keep bits of dust from being inhaled into your lungs, where they might injure delicate tissues. Your nasal passages also warm or cool the air you breathe so that its temperature comes close to body temperature. At the same time, the air picks up moisture from tissue lining the nose. The moisture helps prevent the lungs from drying out. Each nasal cavity contains an olfactory membrane, a stamp-size patch of cells sensitive to smells. These cells form the beginning of the olfactory system. Chemicals in the things you smell cause a reaction in the cells. The cells send messages along the olfactory nerve to your brain. The brain decodes the messages as smells. Here, flowers stimulate the olfactory membrane. A mixture of other odors enters the nose. Some of these odors, such as the aroma of fresh-baked bread, are pleasant. Others, such as the odor of a skunk, are not pleasant. Your olfactory system can identify thousands of different odors—good and bad.

45

Greatly magnified, a grain of pollen from a hollyhock looks like an iron ball studded with spikes (right). Pollen like this can irritate the sensitive lining of your nose, causing a sneeze (below). Sneezing occurs when the muscles that help you breathe suddenly contract. Air bursts from your lungs. It carries the irritating substance away in a cloud of air and water droplets. The cloud can travel at 100 miles an hour (161 km/h)—faster than some hurricane winds.

C. E. MILLER/M. I. T.

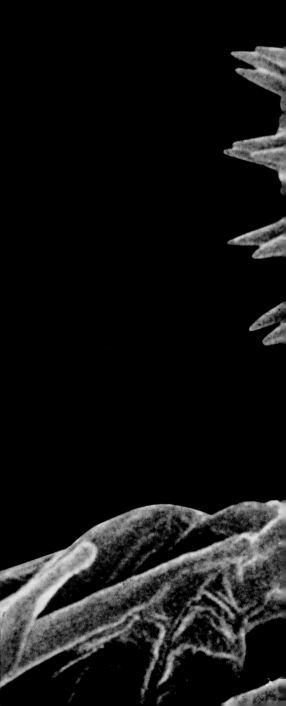

ROZ SCHANZER

Excuse me! Coughs and yawns are reflexes—automatic muscle reactions. If something irritates your windpipe, your cough reflex goes into action. It forces air up from your lungs and expels the irritant. Scientists aren't sure why you yawn. Yawning may be a reflex to supply your body with extra oxygen. Once a yawn starts, you can't stop it. Even if you keep your mouth shut, your muscles will complete the yawn. Try it.

46

BIOPHOTO ASSOCIATES (RIGHT)

1,570 TIMES ACTUAL SIZE

How do I talk?

Speech begins with a breath of air. The air you exhale helps produce sounds. Inside your throat lies your larynx (LAR-inx), or voice box. It's the bump you may know as your Adam's apple. Two springy bands—your vocal cords—stretch from the top of the larynx to the bottom. During normal breathing, they are held apart. When you speak, they come closer together. Muscles in the larynx move the vocal cords.

You make sounds for speaking or singing when air passes through the glottis—the opening between the vocal cords. The air makes the vocal cords vibrate, producing sounds. The motion of your tongue and lips changes the sounds into words. You control the loudness of your voice by changing the amount of air passing through the glottis.

You also use your respiratory system when you sing, whistle, hum, or shout. You use it when you sneeze, cough, cry, laugh, or hiccup, too.

You might not think that your lungs have much to do with laughing, but next time you laugh, notice what happens. You take a deep breath, and let it out in short bursts through the vocal cords. Crying works the same way. If there's a baby in your house, you've probably noticed that the youngster takes a big gulp of air before letting out a wail.

If you play a wind instrument, you also make use of your respiratory system. Most wind instruments—from piccolos to trumpets to tubas—use a stream of air from the lungs to make their sounds.

Your larynx (LAR-inx), or voice box (right), is a delicate instrument. You use it to speak, sing, and laugh. Two vocal cords stretch up and down your larynx. When you speak, muscles bring your vocal cords close together. Air pushed out of your lungs streams past them, producing vibrations that make sounds. You can vary the sounds by changing the tension of the vocal cords. When muscles pull the vocal cords tight, your voice becomes higher. When the vocal cords are loose, your voice is lower. Your mouth, lips, and tongue shape the sounds into words.

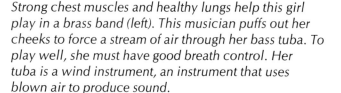

Strong chest muscles and healthy lungs help this girl play in a brass band (left). This musician puffs out her cheeks to force a stream of air through her bass tuba. To play well, she must have good breath control. Her tuba is a wind instrument, an instrument that uses blown air to produce sound.

48

Hiking uses up a lot of energy, as does any other strenuous activity. The harder you exercise, the more energy your cells must produce. Cells need oxygen to produce energy. Oxygen from the air you breathe helps cells generate that energy. You breathe harder when you're exercising than when you're at rest. At rest, you take about 14 breaths a minute. You draw around 2 gallons ($7\frac{1}{2}$ L) of air into your lungs in that minute. During strenuous activity, you may need to fill your lungs with ten times that much air. Your muscle cells signal your brain that they are quickly using up their oxygen. Your brain signals your breathing muscles to make you inhale more deeply and more frequently. That way, your hard-working cells get the oxygen they need.

LOIS SLOAN

4
FUEL
for the body machine

It's lunchtime for these students at Commodore Stockton Elementary School, in San Francisco, California. The food becomes fuel to give them energy for afternoon activities. Their digestive systems change the food into chemical particles to feed the cells that make up every part of their bodies. Below, Bod Squad members—and some peas and corn—enter the stomach. Digestive juices drench the vegetables and help turn them into materials that the body cells can absorb.

veryone needs food to live. It's the fuel that keeps your body going, just as gasoline or diesel fuel keeps an automobile going. A car's fuel gauge warns the driver when the tank needs filling. Your body has a way of warning you when you need more fuel. It makes you feel hungry.

You need energy for everything you do. You need it to run, to laugh, to think, even to dream. Food contains chemical substances called nutrients. Your body needs nutrients not only for energy but also for growth and repair. To enable your cells to absorb nutrients, your body breaks the food into usable parts. This process is called digestion. It starts as soon as you take the first bite.

Let's say you are eating your favorite sandwich. As your teeth bite into the food and grind it, saliva floods your mouth. Saliva makes the food moist and soft for easy swallowing. The saliva also contains enzymes. While the food is still in your mouth, the enzymes begin their job of breaking it down chemically.

As you swallow, the food moves down a long tube to your stomach. The tube is called the esophagus (ih-SOF-uh-gus). Muscles in the stomach mix acid and enzymes with the food. The partially digested food, now a thick liquid, moves into your small intestine. There, two things happen. First, food is further broken down into nutrients. Second, nutrients pass into the bloodstream. The bloodstream carries the nutrients to all your cells.

Particles from the sandwich that your body does not absorb pass into the large intestine. From there, they leave the body as waste.

Small bumps cover your tongue. Among them, too tiny to see here, lie taste buds. The buds send signals to the taste center in your brain.

How does food get into my bloodstream?

Your digestive system breaks food into smaller and smaller particles. It also breaks the food down into its separate chemical parts. Food ends up as nutrient particles smaller than molecules of the food itself.

Millions of bumps shaped like fingers cover the lining of the small intestine. These bumps, called villi (VILL-eye), help absorb the nutrient particles. Networks of capillaries lie inside the villi. The nutrients pass through the thin capillary walls into the bloodstream. Before getting to their final destination, the cells, the nutrients make an important stop in the liver.

Why is my liver important?

Your liver is your body's largest internal organ. It is also your body's main chemical factory. The liver makes bile, a substance that helps digest fat. It manufactures other substances the body needs, as well. It also acts as a filter to remove poisonous materials from the blood.

The liver does one of its most important jobs when it receives blood that is rich in newly digested nutrients. The liver changes some of these nutrients into a material called glucose.

All your cells use glucose for quick energy. Brain cells rely entirely on glucose to keep working. The liver stores material for making glucose. It releases glucose when cells need an extra supply. The liver acts as a kind of bank for your body. It stores vitamins and minerals that you need to stay healthy.

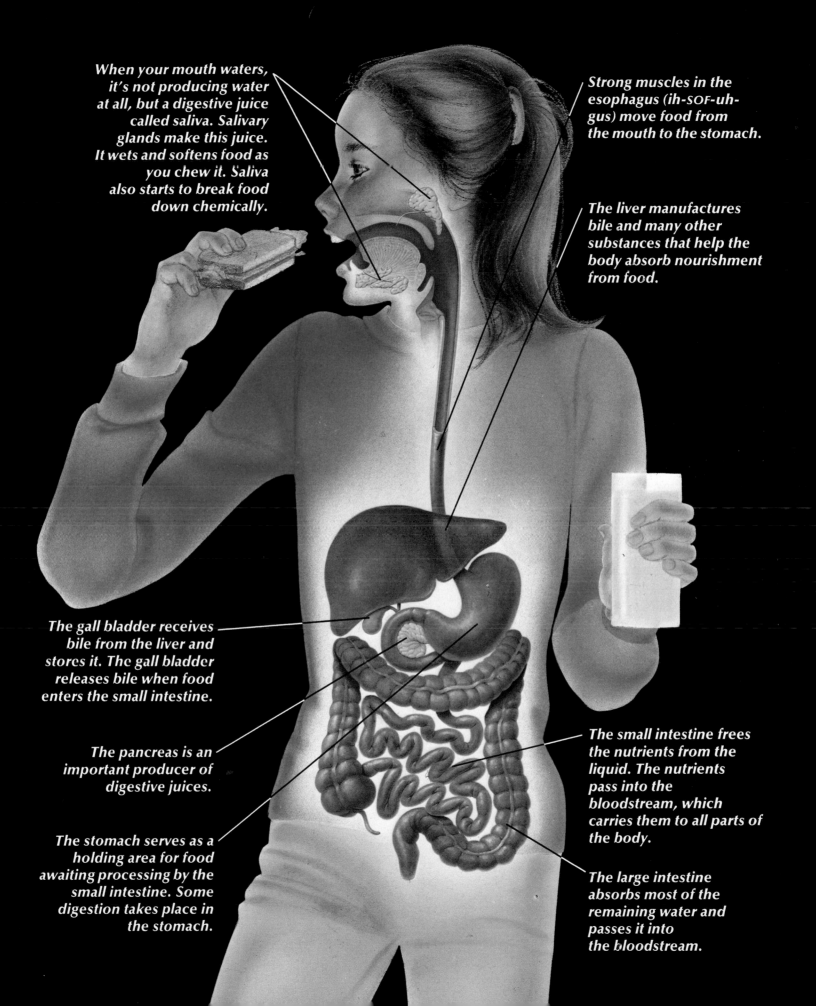

When your mouth waters, it's not producing water at all, but a digestive juice called saliva. Salivary glands make this juice. It wets and softens food as you chew it. Saliva also starts to break food down chemically.

Strong muscles in the esophagus (ih-SOF-uh-gus) move food from the mouth to the stomach.

The liver manufactures bile and many other substances that help the body absorb nourishment from food.

The gall bladder receives bile from the liver and stores it. The gall bladder releases bile when food enters the small intestine.

The pancreas is an important producer of digestive juices.

The stomach serves as a holding area for food awaiting processing by the small intestine. Some digestion takes place in the stomach.

The small intestine frees the nutrients from the liquid. The nutrients pass into the bloodstream, which carries them to all parts of the body.

The large intestine absorbs most of the remaining water and passes it into the bloodstream.

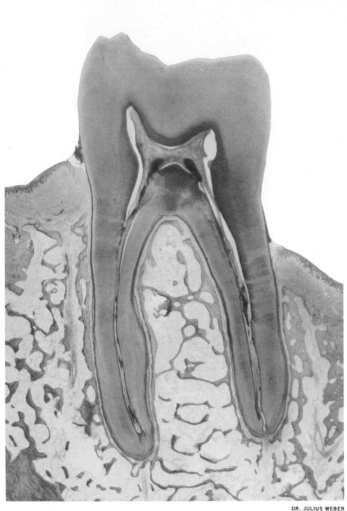

To resist the force of chewing, teeth sit firmly rooted to the jaw. This cutaway view of a single molar shows the layers of the tooth. Enamel, the hardest material in your body, covers the tooth. It protects a softer layer called dentin. Pulp in the center of the tooth contains nerves and blood vessels.

DR. JULIUS WEBER

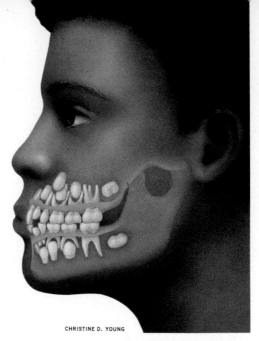

CHRISTINE D. YOUNG

Two sets of teeth seem to crowd a boy's jaw. The baby teeth grew in during his first two years of life. Permanent teeth grew in above and below them. As this boy becomes older, his jaw will become larger. The permanent teeth—usually 32 in all—will replace his 20 baby teeth. Here, some replacement has begun.

Why did my baby teeth fall out?

When you were born and while you were a baby, you probably had no visible teeth at all. But once you began eating solid food, you needed teeth for chewing. One by one, 20 baby teeth—all your small jaws had room for—appeared. As your need for solid foods increased, your jaw grew to make room for larger, more efficient teeth. Your permanent teeth (usually 32 of them) formed near the roots of your baby teeth. The permanent teeth began pushing against the baby teeth when you were about 6. The baby teeth began falling out, and the permanent teeth appeared. Your last permanent teeth, the so-called wisdom teeth, may not appear until you're around 21 years old—or perhaps not at all.

ROZ SCHANZER

By brushing and flossing, this girl protects her teeth. Bacteria, germs present in the mouth, feed on trapped food. They change parts of the food into acid. Unless the acid is removed regularly, it eats into tooth enamel, causing cavities.

N.G.S. PHOTOGRAPHER OTIS IMBODEN

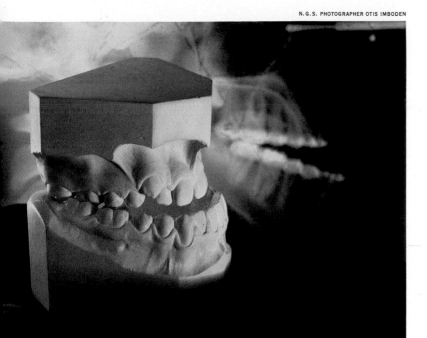

1. An orthodontist, a dentist who specializes in straightening teeth, made these plaster models (above and right). They show the mouth of one of her patients. The patient, a teenage boy, had an alignment problem called an underbite (above). The teeth did not mesh together properly when he bit into something. His lower jaw stuck out.

2. After treatment, the patient had a good bite (below). The orthodontist used braces to pull the teeth into new positions. An operation corrected the jaw problem. The treatment took several years. Braces can improve more than a person's appearance. Properly aligned teeth stay healthy longer. They are easier to clean and are more effective for chewing food than are teeth that do not line up properly.

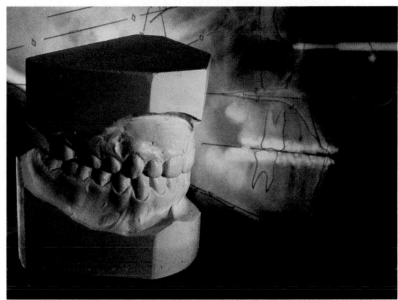

Why do I have different kinds of teeth?

You have four kinds of teeth in your mouth. Each kind has its own job to do. Your front teeth, called incisors (in-SIZE-ers), do the biting. They are thin and sharp. Your four pointed teeth, called canines (KAY-nines), lie next to the incisors. They look somewhat like a dog's sharp teeth. In fact, "canine" is another word for "dog." These teeth help in cutting and tearing food, especially meat.

Next to the canine teeth lie broad teeth called premolars. These eight teeth help in grinding food, making the food easier to swallow. Next come the back teeth, the molars. These are the largest teeth in the mouth. Your molars do most of the grinding as you chew food.

The next time you eat something, pay attention to the way your teeth work. You'll notice, for instance, that you use your incisors to bite into an apple. Then your tongue moves the bite of apple back to your grinding teeth for chewing.

Your back teeth should fit together when you chew and when you close your jaws. If they don't, or if your teeth are crooked, dentists can put on braces to straighten the teeth.

Gradually, over about two years, the braces move the teeth into the correct position for biting and chewing.

What's the best way to brush my teeth — up and down, or sideways?

Dentists don't agree on this question. Some say the up-and-down method gets your teeth cleaner. Others say that brushing sideways works better. Dentists do agree that the most important thing is to give your teeth a really thorough cleaning. You should brush vigorously for at least three minutes twice a day. You should also use dental floss regularly—at least once a day.

Brushing and flossing remove bacteria and food particles from the mouth. Bacteria are germs. They interact with certain foods—especially sugar—to produce acid. The acid eats into the hard, shiny enamel that covers your teeth, causing decay. Removing food particles and bacteria promptly by proper brushing and flossing can help you prevent decay.

55

SOUR
BITTER

SWEET

SWEET,
SALTY

CHRISTINE D. YOUNG

When you take a bite of food, your taste buds send information about its taste to your brain. You can taste things with most parts of your mouth (left). That's because bumps called papillae (puh-PILL-ee) cover the top of your tongue, the roof of your mouth, and the back of your throat. Papillae contain taste buds. The buds react to four tastes: sweetness, sourness, bitterness, and saltiness. Different parts of your mouth are more sensitive to certain tastes than other parts are. The front two-thirds of your tongue is most sensitive to sweet and salty tastes. The back third reacts most strongly to sweetness. Taste buds on the roof of your mouth react the most to bitter and sour foods.

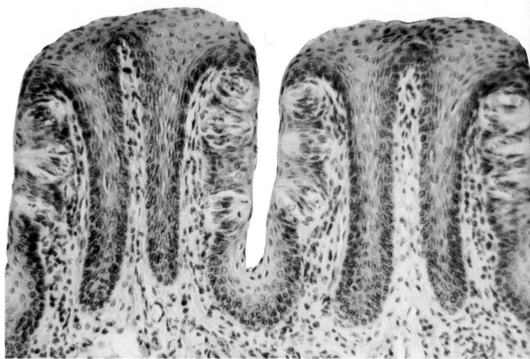

Through a microscope, papillae on the tongue look like peaks and valleys (right). Egg-shaped taste buds line the sides of the papillae. Your sense of taste works with your senses of smell and sight. Together these senses enable you to taste different flavors.

1,082 TIMES ACTUAL SIZE

DR. JULIUS WEBER

How does my nose help my sense of taste?

Your nose gives your sense of taste a big boost. You have thousands of taste buds in your mouth. They react to chemicals in food and send taste messages to the brain. Your taste buds tell you that things are sweet, sour, bitter, or salty, or are combinations of these tastes. But your more delicate sense of smell can detect many more differences. Have you ever eaten a favorite food when you had a bad cold? You probably noticed that the food didn't have much flavor. That's because the cold stuffed up your nose and took away your sense of smell. Your taste buds had to work alone.

Your vision apparently plays a part in taste, as well. Orange juice, for example, tastes more like orange juice if you see it. The relationship between sight and taste is probably indirect. Seeing a food helps you to anticipate a flavor, rather than actually to taste it.

You use your combined senses of taste and smell to enjoy the many different flavors of food. You also use these senses to tell if food is spoiled. Think of what you do if you fear the milk in your refrigerator may be going sour. First you sniff it. If you're still not sure, you carefully take a sip. Your ancient ancestors probably relied on the senses of taste and smell for survival. If something they gathered from a plant tasted bad, they spat it out. The bad flavor helped to protect them from being poisoned by unfamiliar fruits and berries.

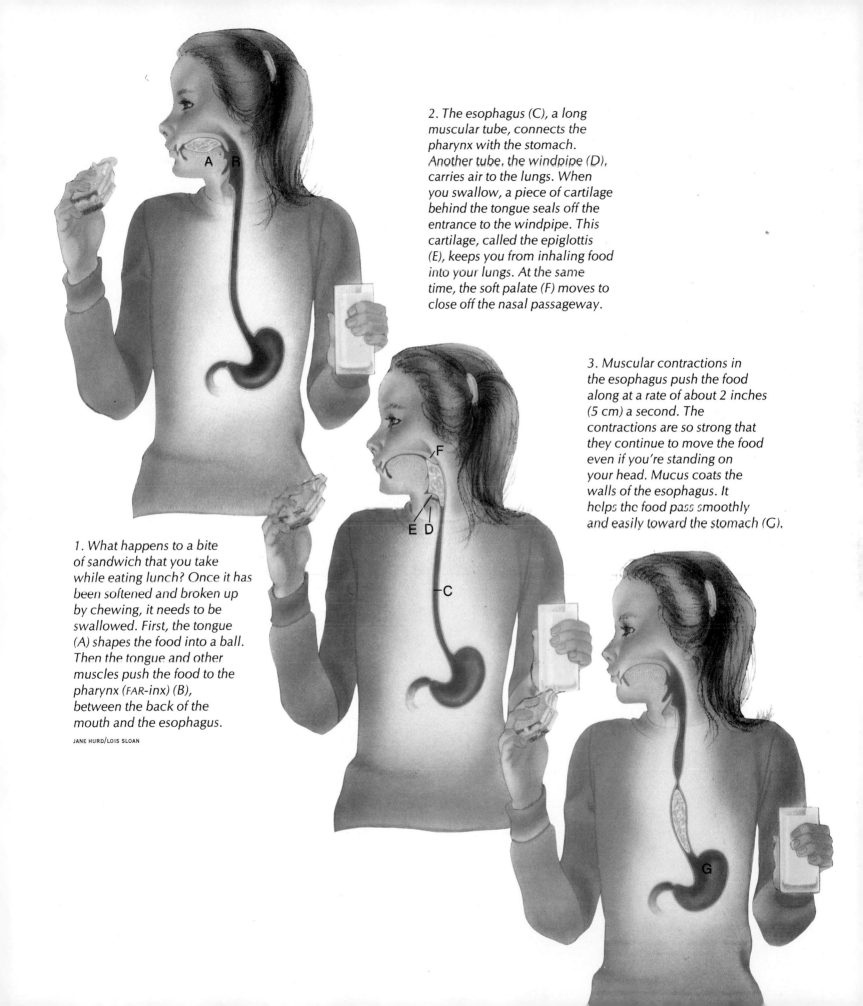

2. The esophagus (C), a long muscular tube, connects the pharynx with the stomach. Another tube, the windpipe (D), carries air to the lungs. When you swallow, a piece of cartilage behind the tongue seals off the entrance to the windpipe. This cartilage, called the epiglottis (E), keeps you from inhaling food into your lungs. At the same time, the soft palate (F) moves to close off the nasal passageway.

3. Muscular contractions in the esophagus push the food along at a rate of about 2 inches (5 cm) a second. The contractions are so strong that they continue to move the food even if you're standing on your head. Mucus coats the walls of the esophagus. It helps the food pass smoothly and easily toward the stomach (G).

1. What happens to a bite of sandwich that you take while eating lunch? Once it has been softened and broken up by chewing, it needs to be swallowed. First, the tongue (A) shapes the food into a ball. Then the tongue and other muscles push the food to the pharynx (FAR-inx) (B), between the back of the mouth and the esophagus.

JANE HURD/LOIS SLOAN

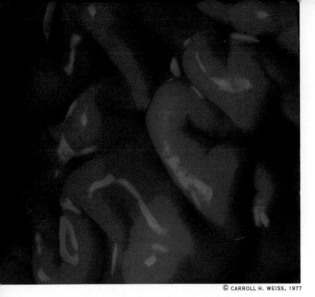

Crumpled folds make up the inner lining of the stomach. The stomach holds food until the small intestine is ready to process it. As you eat, your stomach enlarges. The folds smooth out, making more room for food.

Does your stomach sometimes embarrass you by growling (above)? It makes noises when muscles churn an empty stomach. When you're hungry, just thinking about food can start the sound effects.

Fingerlike bumps called villi (VILL-eye) cover the inner surface of the small intestine (below). This photograph magnifies the villi many times. Each one of the villi in the small intestine contains a network of blood vessels called capillaries. Nutrients from food pass through the thin walls of the villi into the bloodstream. Once in the blood, the nutrients travel to other cells in the body.

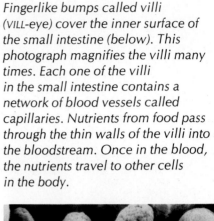

95 TIMES ACTUAL SIZE

The liver and gall bladder lie close together. The egg-shaped organ is the gall bladder. Part of the liver shows to the left of the gall bladder. Cells in the liver make bile, which the gall bladder stores. Bile breaks fat into small droplets. Then enzymes break down the droplets into chemical particles.

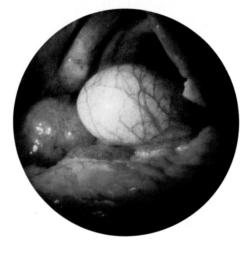

The food you eat makes its last stop in the large intestine (right). A computer has added color to this X ray. Most of the water left over in the digestive process will return to the body from the large intestine. Bacteria digest remaining bits of food. Materials that the body cannot use collect in the large intestine to be expelled as waste.

What happens to food when it reaches my stomach?

Your stomach is a kind of bag, shaped like the letter "J." It acts as a holding tank for food. It expands as you eat. The stomach can hold up to 3 pints (1½ L) of food at any one time.

Muscles in the stomach mix digestive juices with the food. The juices are very strong. They begin to break the food into separate chemicals. The powerful digestive juices don't hurt the stomach because a lining of mucus protects it.

Sometimes your stomach begins its work even though you haven't eaten. That's when you feel and hear the rumblings and gurglings that signal hunger. The cells that produce digestive juices in your stomach may go into action whether you've eaten or not. Seeing or smelling food—even thinking about it—can stimulate your stomach into producing digestive juices and making churning noises.

It takes from two to six hours for your stomach to empty itself. Some foods take longer to pass through the stomach than others. Carbohydrates, such as potatoes or corn, leave first. It takes longer for a meal with fats, such as sausages or pork chops, to pass through the stomach.

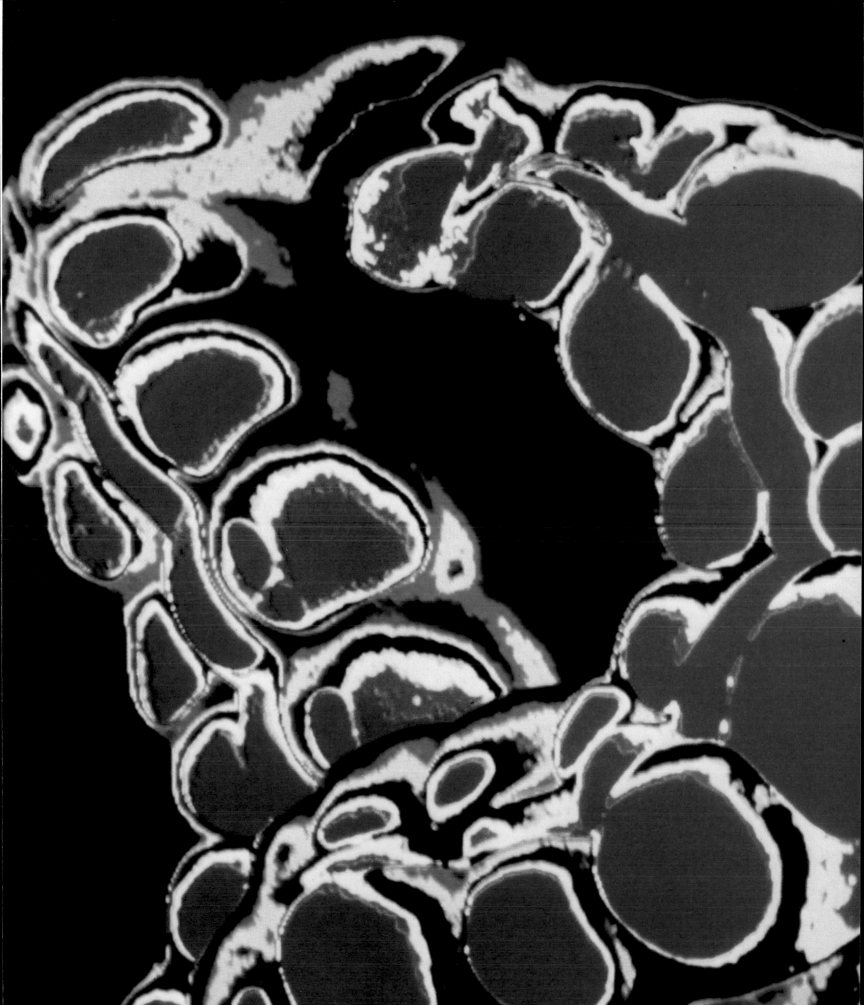

On a picnic, youngsters choose from a variety of foods from the five basic food groups: 1. Milk and milk products provide the calcium needed for strong bones. 2. Meat, beans, and nuts provide protein for growth. 3. Whole-grain bread and cereal contain carbohydrates, a source of energy. 4. Fruit and vegetables provide vitamins, which help preserve health. 5. Sweets and fats provide energy but few nutrients. Don't overdo sweets and fats.

What is a well-balanced diet, and why do people say it's so important?

To function at its best, your body needs a variety of nutrients. Each nutrient has an important job to do. A well-balanced diet is a diet that provides all the nutrients. It contains foods from five basic groups (above). If you eat a well-balanced diet, you can be sure of getting the nutrients you need.

Scientists list six groups of nutrients. They are carbohydrates, fats, proteins, vitamins, minerals, and water.

Carbohydrates and fats provide the energy that your cells need to carry out their work. That energy helps you do everything from thinking up riddles to running races.

For growth, your body needs proteins, the chemicals that form muscle, skin, and hair. Proteins also help keep your body in repair by forming new red blood cells to replace cells that wear out.

Vitamins and minerals help regulate the body's chemical activity. A well-balanced diet of fresh, healthful foods provides all the vitamins and minerals most people need.

Finally, you need water. About two-thirds of your body is water. You can't live long without it. Water carries nutrients to the cells. It also aids in such processes as temperature regulation and waste disposal.

As Cham Giobbi, 14, of Katonah, New York, cuts a slice of bread, his mother tosses a fresh green salad. Iron from whole grains in the bread and in the dark, leafy vegetables helps build strong red blood cells. Vitamins in the fresh greens will increase Cham's resistance to infection and help keep him healthy. These foods also contain plant fiber, which aids in the disposal of body waste.

As you move and grow, your body uses units of energy called calories. Your food supplies the calories. Different activities use up different amounts of calories. The youngsters at this picnic are using energy at different rates. While sitting, the boy burns up 80 to 100 calories an hour. The girl walking and carrying the thermos uses 120 to 240 calories an hour. The boy racing along on his bike uses the most energy. His vigorous exercise burns up 250 to 350 calories an hour. To stay healthy, your body should take in about the same number of calories that it burns up. If you take in too few calories, your body will burn up the energy stored in your cells without replacing it. You may become underweight. If you eat more calories than you burn, you may become overweight.

ROZ SCHANZER

5

the
HEART
of the matter

Winning runner Tommy Howze and runner-up Tom Wilde, both 10 and both of Arlington, Virginia, can feel their hearts racing at the finish line. As the muscles work harder, they need more oxygen. Blood must deliver enough oxygen to help support hardworking muscle cells. To do this job, blood must flow continuously through the body. The heart keeps this flow going. Below, Bod Squad members hitch rides on red blood cells, which carry oxygen to the body's other cells.

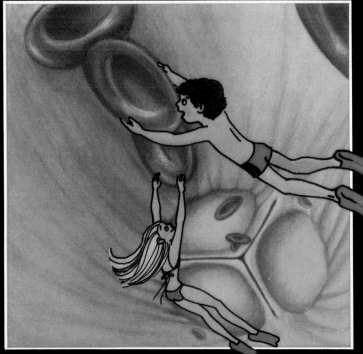

JOYCE HURWITZ/ROZ SCHANZER

MATTHEW NEAL McVAY (LEFT)

63

You're probably sitting quietly as you read this book, yet your body continues to work hard. Your heart, the most vital muscle in your body, beats regularly as you read. You can feel its *lub-dub lub-dub* rhythm if you place your hand on the left side of your chest. That familiar heartbeat keeps blood flowing through your body, delivering oxygen and nutrients to your cells.

What does my heart look like?

What it *doesn't* look like is the heart on a valentine. The heart is actually about the same shape and size as a fist. It weighs slightly less than a pound ($\frac{1}{2}$ kg).

Your heart is mostly hollow. A thick wall of muscle called the septum divides the heart into right and left halves. On both sides of the septum lie two chambers, one above the other. The upper chamber on each side is called an atrium (AY-tree-um). Each lower chamber is called a ventricle. The atriums serve as storage places for blood flowing into the heart. The ventricles pump blood out of the heart. Valves connect the chambers, allowing blood to flow from each atrium to the ventricle below it. Two other valves release blood to vessels leading away from the ventricles.

What makes my heart beat?

A small area of specialized tissue inside your heart keeps the heart beating. The tissue, called the pacemaker, gives off a small electrical impulse about 70 times a minute. The impulse excites the tissue, causing it to contract. The contractions

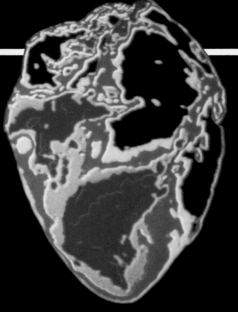

Day in and day out, your heart pumps blood through your circulatory system. In a normal lifetime, this strong muscle will beat about $2\frac{1}{2}$ billion times. Color has been added to this picture.

result in heartbeats. Valves, as they snap open and shut, make the *lub-dub* sound.

What does my heartbeat do?

Each heartbeat sends blood flowing one step farther along a complex circuit of blood vessels. The vessels, together with the heart, make up the circulatory system.

Your heart beats 100,000 times a day without ever resting. A lot happens during each heartbeat. First, the two upper chambers, the atriums, relax and fill with blood. The left atrium receives oxygen-rich blood from the lungs. The right atrium receives oxygen-poor blood from the rest of the body. Then the electrical impulse set off by the pacemaker spreads through each atrium. The impulse causes each atrium to contract. This action forces blood into the ventricles.

The impulse then moves downward to the ventricles. It spreads across the ventricles, causing them to contract. This squeeze pushes blood from the right ventricle through a large artery into the lungs. There the blood absorbs oxygen. The same contraction sends blood spurting out of the left ventricle and into the aorta (ay-ORT-uh). This large vessel starts oxygen-rich blood on its way throughout your circulatory system.

What *is* blood?

Every part of your body depends on blood. This red fluid bathes and nourishes body tissues. It carries oxygen and nutrients to body cells. It also carries away waste products from the cells. It fights

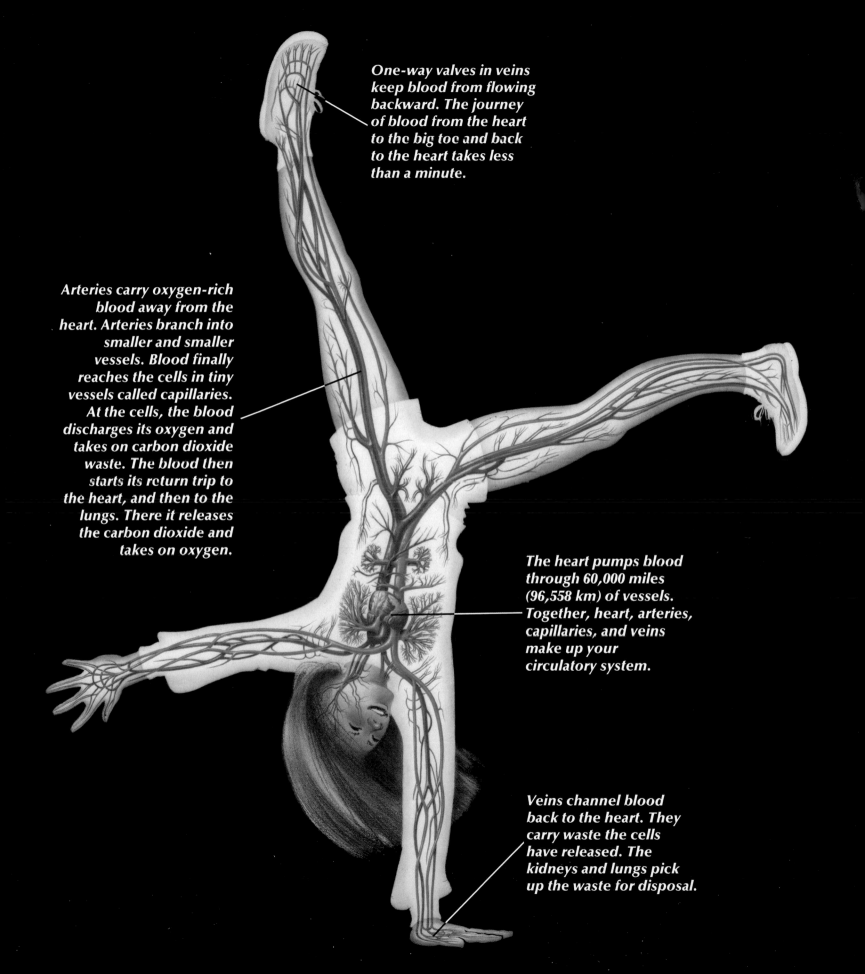

One-way valves in veins keep blood from flowing backward. The journey of blood from the heart to the big toe and back to the heart takes less than a minute.

Arteries carry oxygen-rich blood away from the heart. Arteries branch into smaller and smaller vessels. Blood finally reaches the cells in tiny vessels called capillaries. At the cells, the blood discharges its oxygen and takes on carbon dioxide waste. The blood then starts its return trip to the heart, and then to the lungs. There it releases the carbon dioxide and takes on oxygen.

The heart pumps blood through 60,000 miles (96,558 km) of vessels. Together, heart, arteries, capillaries, and veins make up your circulatory system.

Veins channel blood back to the heart. They carry waste the cells have released. The kidneys and lungs pick up the waste for disposal.

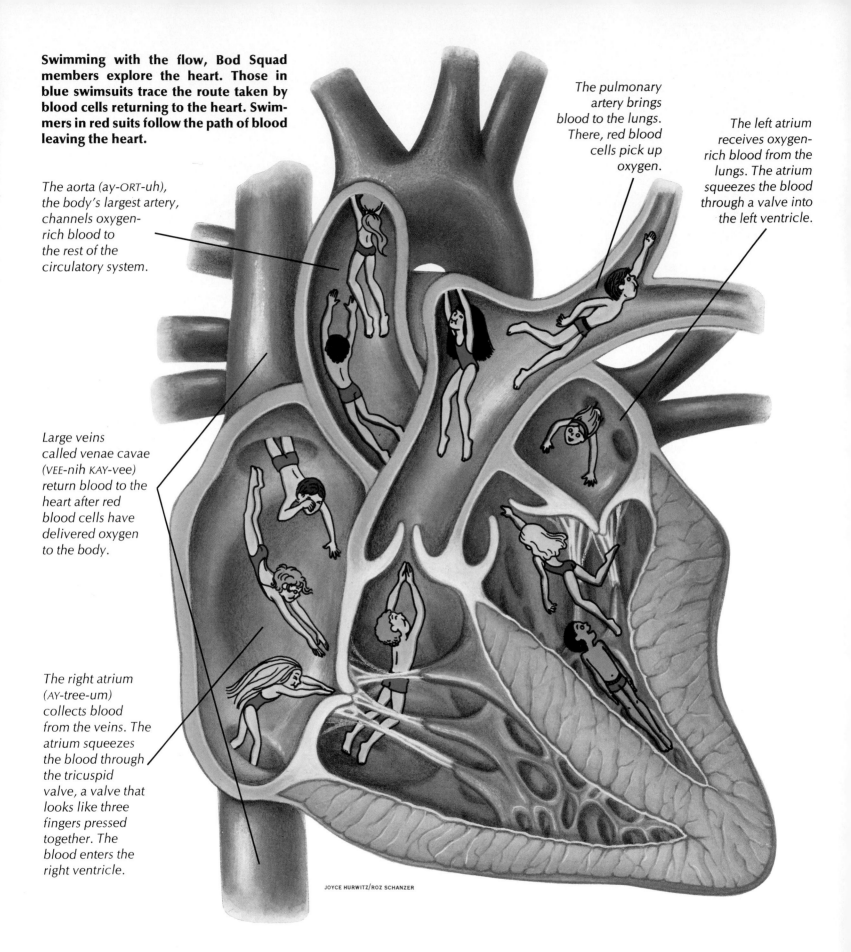

Swimming with the flow, Bod Squad members explore the heart. Those in blue swimsuits trace the route taken by blood cells returning to the heart. Swimmers in red suits follow the path of blood leaving the heart.

The pulmonary artery brings blood to the lungs. There, red blood cells pick up oxygen.

The left atrium receives oxygen-rich blood from the lungs. The atrium squeezes the blood through a valve into the left ventricle.

The aorta (ay-ORT-uh), the body's largest artery, channels oxygen-rich blood to the rest of the circulatory system.

Large veins called venae cavae (VEE-nih KAY-vee) return blood to the heart after red blood cells have delivered oxygen to the body.

The right atrium (AY-tree-um) collects blood from the veins. The atrium squeezes the blood through the tricuspid valve, a valve that looks like three fingers pressed together. The blood enters the right ventricle.

JOYCE HURWITZ/ROZ SCHANZER

disease-causing germs that invade your body. It helps keep your body temperature at around 98.6°F (37.0°C)—the temperature at which your organs function best.

What is blood made of?

Blood consists of four main parts. They are red cells, white cells, platelets, and plasma. Red blood cells carry oxygen throughout your body. White blood cells fight germs that cause disease. Platelets help heal cuts.

Plasma makes up slightly more than half of each drop of blood. It looks like a yellowish syrup. It contains hundreds of chemicals, including proteins, minerals, and sugars. Proteins repair damaged cells and build new tissues. Minerals, such as calcium, help keep your bones strong and your teeth in good repair. Minerals also help other organs do their jobs. Sugars give you energy.

How much blood do I have?

When you were born, your body contained about three-quarters of a pint (355 ml) of blood. As a teenager, you have about a gallon (4 L) of blood flowing through your circulatory system. As an adult, you'll have only slightly more than that. The exact amount of blood you have depends largely on your size and weight. The larger and heavier you are, the more blood your body carries.

Your total blood supply lies in your circulatory system. You do have a back-up supply of red blood cells, however. It is contained in the liver and in the spleen, an organ under the diaphragm. When the blood needs red cells quickly, the liver and the spleen release their supply into the bloodstream. You do not have a back-up supply of white blood cells. When disease germs invade, the body can rapidly manufacture the white cells it needs to fight them.

Where you live plays a role in the number of red cells your blood contains—though not in the total amount of the blood itself. If you live high on a mountain, you have more red blood cells than a person who lives in the lowlands has. There is less oxygen at high altitude than at low altitude. Less oxygen means your body must make extra red cells to capture the oxygen you need.

Why is my blood red?

A drop of blood contains about five million red blood cells. This high number of cells makes your blood look red. White blood cells aren't really white. They are transparent, so they don't add color to your blood.

A substance called hemoglobin (HEE-muh-glow-bin) gives the red blood cells their color. Hemoglobin contains iron. When the oxygen in the air you breathe meets the iron in hemoglobin, a chemical change takes place. It causes blood cells to turn bright red.

MARTIN ROGERS

Darrick Day, 15, of Arlington, Virginia, takes his pulse after running. Each heartbeat advances blood through the bloodstream. Each heartbeat results in a thump downstream—the pulse. You can feel your pulse where arteries are close to the skin surface, as they are on the undersides of your wrists. Your pulse tells you how fast your heart is beating. It can help you pace yourself when you exercise. When you're at rest, your heart beats between 60 and 80 times a minute. When you exercise, it can climb much higher. During exercise breaks, you can check your heart rate by taking your pulse. Place two fingers lightly over a spot where you can feel your pulse. Your wrists or the sides of your neck are the best places. Count the number of times your heart beats in 60 seconds. This will tell you how much the exercise has increased your heart rate. During vigorous exercise, your heart might race at a rate of 200 beats a minute—or even slightly more.

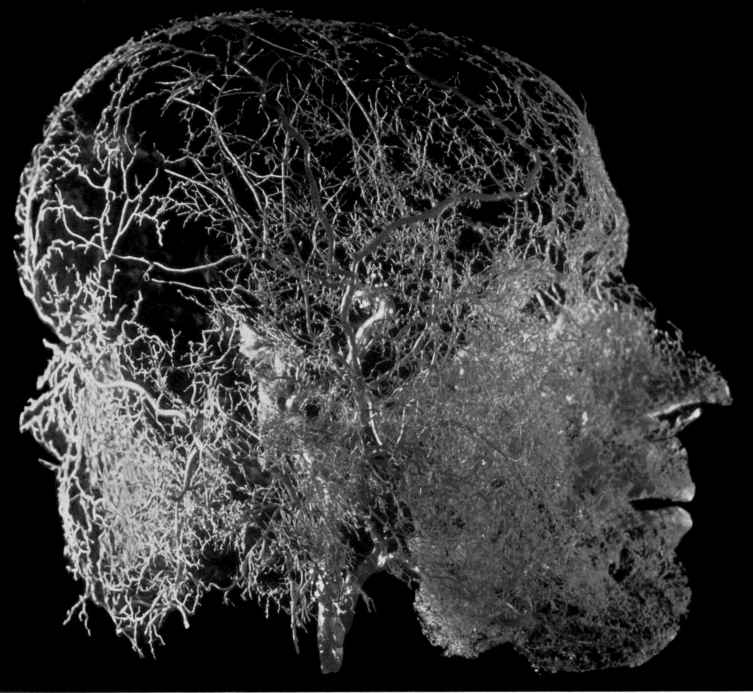

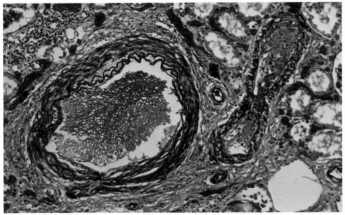

260 TIMES ACTUAL SIZE

A web of blood vessels laces the human head, as this plastic cast (above) shows. An ample flow of blood to the head is vital. The brain makes up only about 2 percent of total body weight, but it uses 15 percent of the oxygen the body takes in.

A cross-section of an artery and a vein shows differences in the vessels' walls. The thick walls of the artery, left, can stand up to the high pressure of blood spurting from the heart. The vein, here shaped somewhat like a bow tie, doesn't need so thick a wall. Pressure in the veins is lower than pressure in the arteries.

Your blood isn't always the same shade of red. As red blood cells give up their oxygen to body cells, they pick up carbon dioxide waste. This exchange causes another chemical action. The bright red blood cells that left your heart to journey through your body become darker and more purplish during their trip back to your heart.

How does blood move through my body?

Every time your heart beats, your blood begins a journey through 60,000 miles of blood vessels (96,558 km) —enough to stretch $2\frac{1}{2}$ times around the earth. Arteries leading from the heart carry blood into small vessels called arterioles (are-TEER-ee-ohls). Arterioles branch into your body's smallest vessels, the capillaries. Capillaries lie near every one of the trillions of cells that form your body. Ten capillaries bundled together would be only about as thick as a human hair. Capillaries are so narrow that your blood cells can flow inside them only one cell at a time.

Capillary walls are only a single cell thick. The oxygen and nutrients in your blood pass right through the walls and into the other cells of your body. At the same time, carbon dioxide and other waste products of the cells pass into the blood, eventually to be expelled from the body.

Capillaries join to form larger vessels called venules (VEN-yules). Venules form into veins, which lead back toward the right side of the heart. The heart pumps the blood to the lungs. There, the blood releases carbon dioxide and picks up oxygen. The oxygen-rich blood returns to the heart at its left side. The cycle begins again.

Can my blood flow backward?

No, it can't. In your arteries, the constant pressure produced by the heartbeat keeps your blood flowing in one direction only. Throughout your system of veins, valves make sure that your blood doesn't back up. Valves work like one-way doors. They open when blood comes through them. Then they close. No blood can get back through in the other direction.

Valves inside your heart allow blood to flow from one chamber to another. A valve connects your right ventricle with the artery that leads to your lungs. Another valve connects the left ventricle to the aorta. These valves open when blood is pumped into the arteries. They close when the arteries fill up. When a doctor listens to your heart with a stethoscope, he hears the sound of the heart valves opening and closing.

Beads of blood speckle glass rings of a machine that tests blood (above). Human blood can be divided into types. In the classification system most commonly used, there are four blood types: A, B, AB, and O. Your doctor can tell you what type of blood you have. A chemical put in a testing machine makes different types of blood turn different colors. Grouping blood into types makes it possible for doctors to take blood from one person and transfuse, or transfer, it to another person. Doctors know which blood types can be substituted for other types—and which cannot. People who lose blood because of sickness or a bad accident often need a transfusion. The Red Cross and other organizations collect blood so it will be available to people who need it.

ANNIE GRIFFITHS

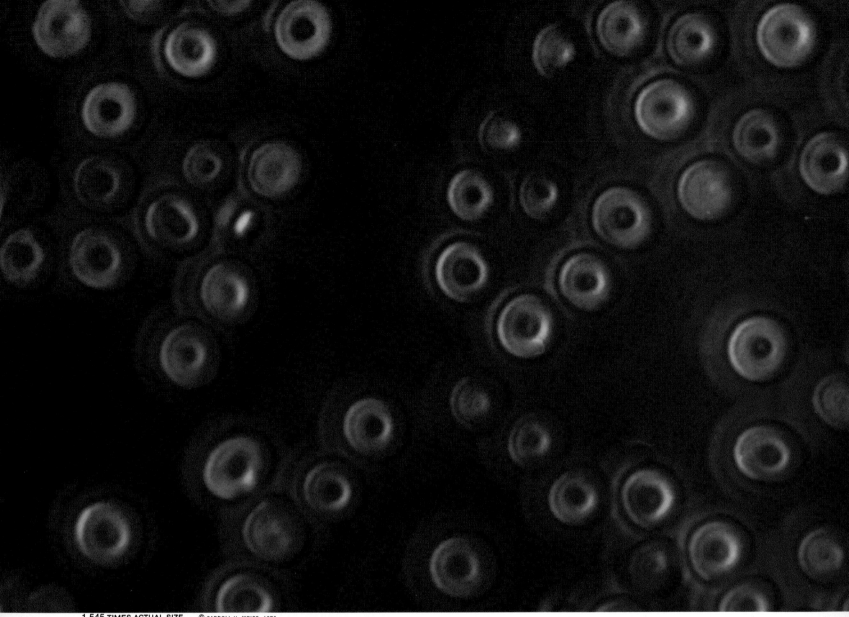

1,545 TIMES ACTUAL SIZE   © CARROLL H. WEISS, 1976

What is blood pressure, and why do doctors check it?

The blood in your circulatory system is constantly pushing against the walls of your blood vessels. A blood-pressure reading shows how hard the liquid is pushing on the walls that hold it in.

Your blood-pressure reading depends on the strength and rate of your heartbeat. It also depends on the flexibility of the walls of your arteries. A blood-pressure reading consists of two numbers, one higher than the other.

Let's say you have a normal blood-pressure reading of 120 over 80. The higher number stands for the amount of pressure your blood puts on your arteries when it spurts out of your heart. It is called systolic pressure. The lower number stands for diastolic pressure—the pressure on the arteries between beats. When your heart is relaxing and filling with blood, the pressure goes down.

By checking your blood pressure, doctors can tell a lot about the condition of your heart and your blood vessels. Pressure that is too high indicates that your heart is straining to pump blood through your body. Such constant strain is bad for the heart.

Fortunately, doctors can control high blood pressure with medication. Even better, they can sometimes prevent the problem in the first place—if you follow their advice. A leading cause of high blood pressure, doctors say, is too much salt in the diet. They recommend that people go easy with the saltshaker at mealtime.

A stain of color added to white blood cells makes the cells visible under a microscope (below). White blood cells are actually transparent. These cells work as watchdogs in your bloodstream. They guard your health by fighting harmful germs that find their way into your body.

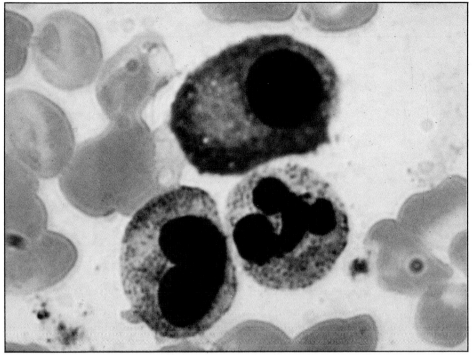

MARILYN J. KOERING

2,500 TIMES ACTUAL SIZE

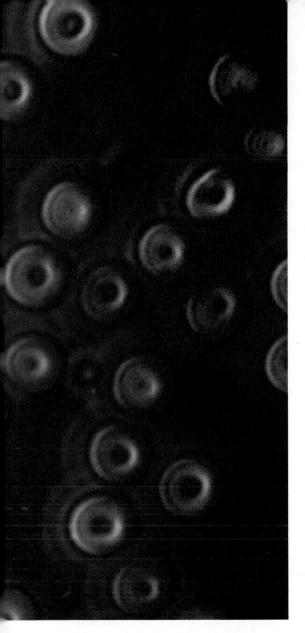

Shaped like buttons, red blood cells crowd against each other (above). Millions of these cells fill each drop of your blood. Red cells, which carry oxygen to your other cells, live for about 120 days. When they wear out, new ones take their place. Tissue in your bones produces red and white blood cells.

WORDS FROM THE HEART. You may say "I'm heartbroken" when you feel sad. You may call a mean person "cold-blooded." The drawings below show some expressions that have to do with your heart and blood.

 Embarrassing moments can send blood rushing to your face, causing a blush. This girl might describe her embarrassment by saying, *"I was red as a beet."*

 Noblemen are often called *blue-blooded.* The phrase started in Spain centuries ago. Many rich people avoided the sun. They thought tanned skin would mark them as commoners. Their skin was so pale that blue veins showed vividly through the surface.

 Generous people, such as this boy sharing his candy, are often described as being *bighearted* or as having *a heart as big as all outdoors.*

 This terrified boy just heard a *blood-curdling scream.* His blood hasn't really curdled, but he may feel as if it has. Some people express feelings of fear by saying, *"My blood ran cold in my veins!"*

ROZ SCHANZER

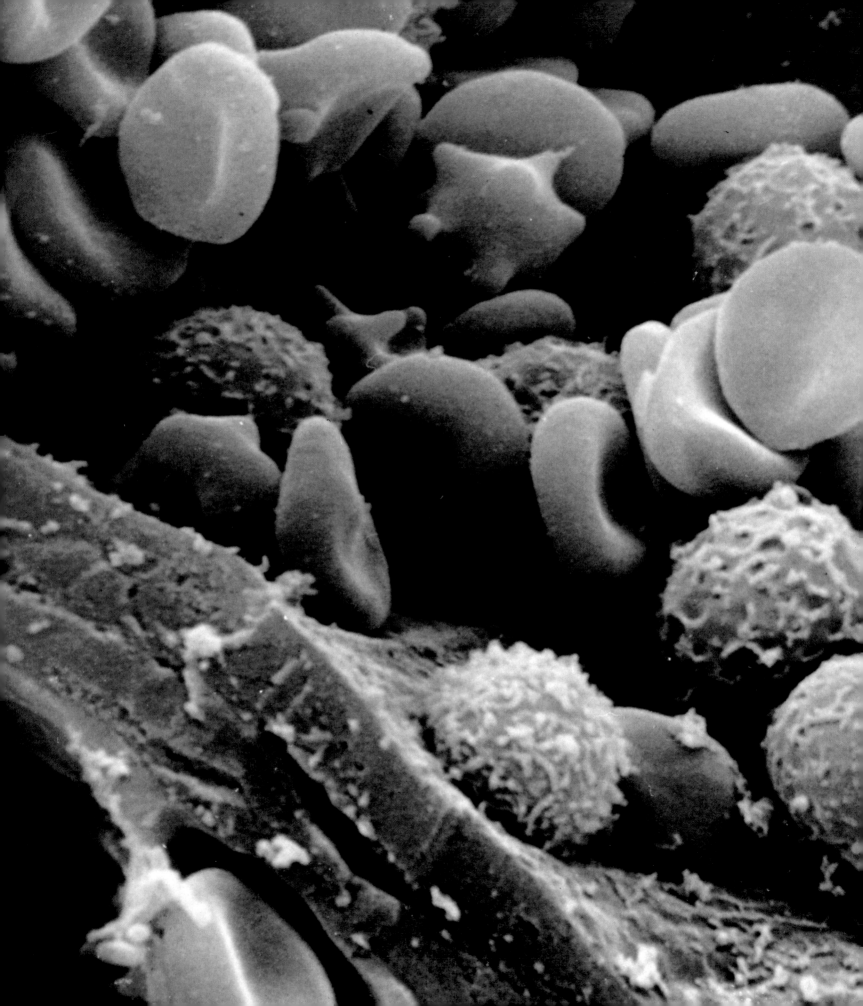

Inside an artery, white blood cells mix with red blood cells. The scooped-out shape of the red cells increases the cells' surface area. This shape enables them to carry more oxygen molecules than they could if they were perfectly flat. A scientist cut open an artery to make this picture. You can see the cut section of the artery wall at lower left.

JOYCE HURWITZ/ROZ SCHANZER

How do I stop bleeding when I cut myself?

Bod Squad members (left) show what happens when you cut or scratch yourself. Here, a cut breaks the skin (A) and a blood vessel (B). The cut causes bleeding. As soon as you cut yourself, jellylike blobs called platelets (C) begin the healing. Millions of platelets from the blood gather at the site of the injury. They form a temporary plug. Next, the platelets, the plasma, and the blood-vessel wall release chemical activators. The activators work with a substance from the plasma called fibrinogen (fie-BRIN-uh-jin) to produce a threadlike material called fibrin. The threads form a net over the break in your blood vessel. Red blood cells (D) and platelets cling to the net, forming a long-term clot. Healing of the blood vessel begins as new cells grow underneath the clot. These cells will mend the injury permanently.

How does my blood get rid of waste?

Your kidneys have the vital job of removing waste products from your blood. As blood circulates through your body, it passes through two large bean-shaped organs (A, in the painting at right). These organs are your kidneys. They lie at the lower back of your rib cage.

Blood enters your kidneys through arteries. It flows into tiny filtering units called nephrons (NEF-ronz). Each kidney contains about a million nephrons. A nephron, enlarged thousands of times, appears in the painting. A tightly packed ball of capillaries in each nephron retains blood cells and some nutrients. The dark red arrow shows the path of blood into a capillary ball. The capillaries release the liquid part of the blood into twisted tubules—small tubes. The liquid contains waste products. The yellow arrows show the path of the waste products. A chemical called urea (you-REE-uh) forms the largest portion of the waste. Urea and the other materials can be poisonous if they build up. The body must get rid of them.

Any useful parts of the liquid pass through the walls of the tubules and back into the capillaries (white arrows). From the capillaries it enters the veins (dark blue arrow). The urea and other waste, dissolved in water, form urine. This liquid passes down the tubules into larger tubes known as ureters (YOUR-uht-erz) (B). These tubes lead to a storage sac called the bladder (C). The bladder holds the urine until it passes out of the body through a tube known as the urethra (you-REE-thruh) (D). Kidneys filter your blood supply hundreds of times a day, producing 1 or 2 quarts (1 or 2 L) of urine.

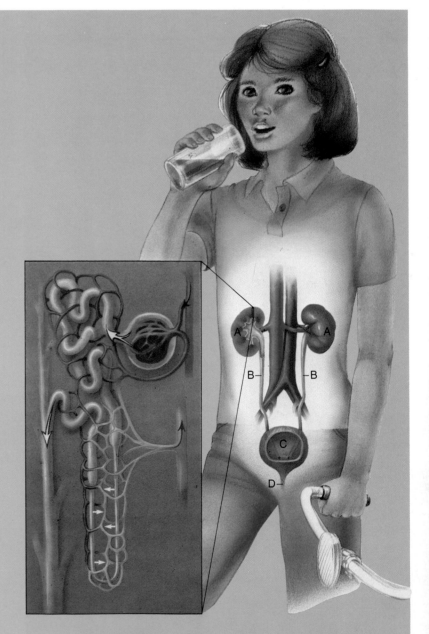

LOIS SLOAN/CHRISTINE D. YOUNG

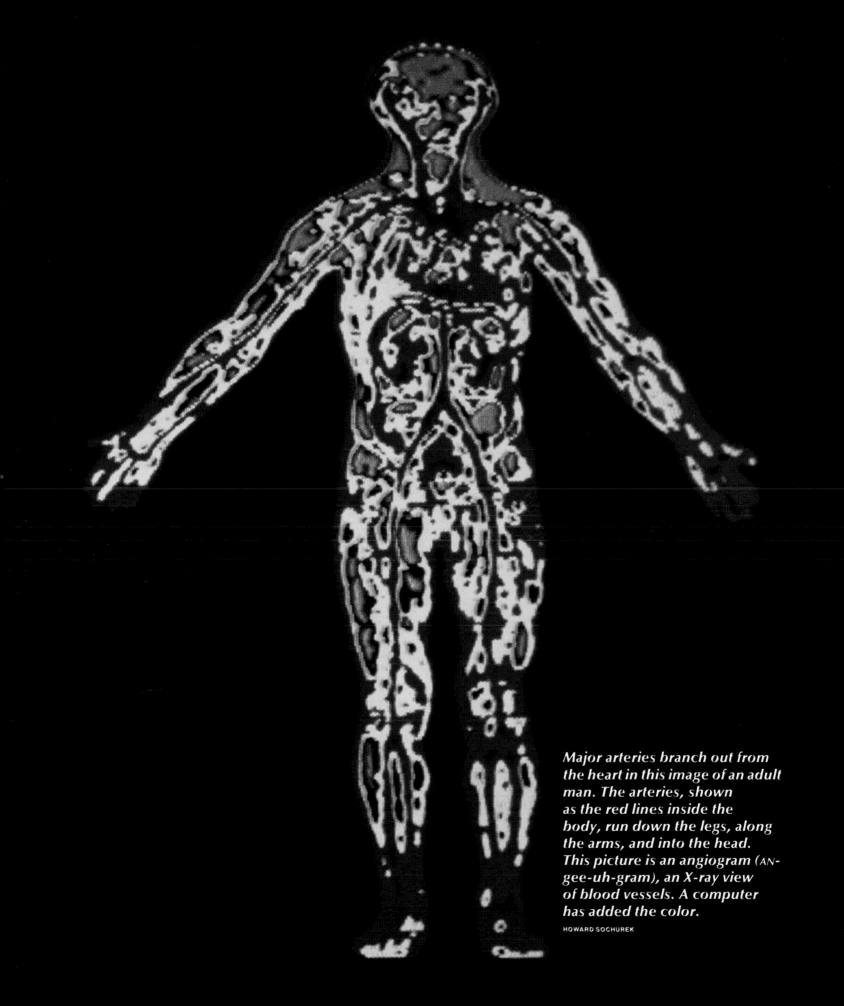

Major arteries branch out from the heart in this image of an adult man. The arteries, shown as the red lines inside the body, run down the legs, along the arms, and into the head. This picture is an angiogram (AN-gee-uh-gram), an X-ray view of blood vessels. A computer has added the color.

6

keep it
MOVING

Racing downhill on skis, Christina Lusse, 18, of Lake Placid, New York, makes a sharp turn. Teamwork between bones and muscles enables her to move her body in many ways. To make this turn, she puts dozens of bones and hundreds of muscles into action. Below, two Bod Squad members climb up a muscle toward a companion on the top of the shinbone. A fourth member slides down the bone. The shinbone is linked to the thighbone at the knee.

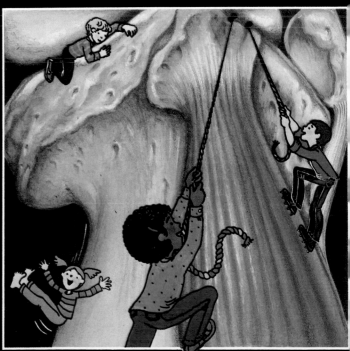

77

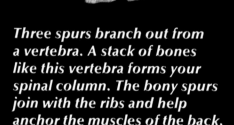

A n acrobat somersaults in the air. A ballerina leaps and lands gracefully on her feet. These movements take strong bones and muscles and a trained body. Even actions that seem simple, such as walking, bending, and kneeling, depend on the body's team of bone and muscle.

Like the framework of a building, your skeleton helps support your body. More than bones make up your skeleton. It also consists of cartilage; of ligaments which bind one bone to another, and of tendons, which join muscle to bone.

The body of the average adult has about 206 bones and about 650 muscles. Working together, bones and muscles help you move in many ways. Working alone, muscles operate your internal organs. Without bones and muscles, your body would be as floppy as that of a jellyfish.

What do my muscles do?

Muscles are the engines of your body. Leg muscles help you run. Chest muscles help you breathe. Stomach muscles mix acids and enzymes with food to help break it down into nutrients. Face muscles help show others your mood — or mask it. Your heart, the busiest of all the muscles, helps keep you alive by pumping blood through your body.

Are all my muscles the same?

No — you actually have three kinds of muscle: skeletal, smooth, and heart. Skeletal muscles are the strongest. They make up the largest part of the muscular system. Skeletal muscles help you to

Three spurs branch out from a vertebra. A stack of bones like this vertebra forms your spinal column. The bony spurs join with the ribs and help anchor the muscles of the back.

swing a baseball bat, to run a race, to strum and pluck a guitar, to build a tiny model airplane. Skeletal muscles do much the same job as the strings on a string puppet. They pull on bones, causing movement.

The second kind of muscle is called smooth muscle. It makes your internal organs, such as your lungs, work. Smooth muscle gets its name from its smooth appearance under a microscope.

Finally, there's heart muscle. Like smooth muscle, heart muscle works without your giving it a thought and without its getting tired. Unlike smooth muscle, however, it resembles striped skeletal muscle under a microscope.

How do my muscles work?

You have different kinds of muscle, but they all work in the same basic way, by contracting and relaxing. Both actions are necessary in doing a particular job. Chest muscles, for example, contract to expand the chest cavity and help you inhale. When they relax, the chest cavity shrinks, helping to force air out. Muscles contract and relax in response to messages from the brain or spinal cord. The messages pass into the muscles you consciously control at a rapid rate—about 50 a second. They pass into other muscles—those that operate without thought—at a slower rate.

What are my bones made of ?

When you were an unborn baby, your skeleton had few bones. Most of your skeleton was made of cartilage. Cartilage contains many minerals. The

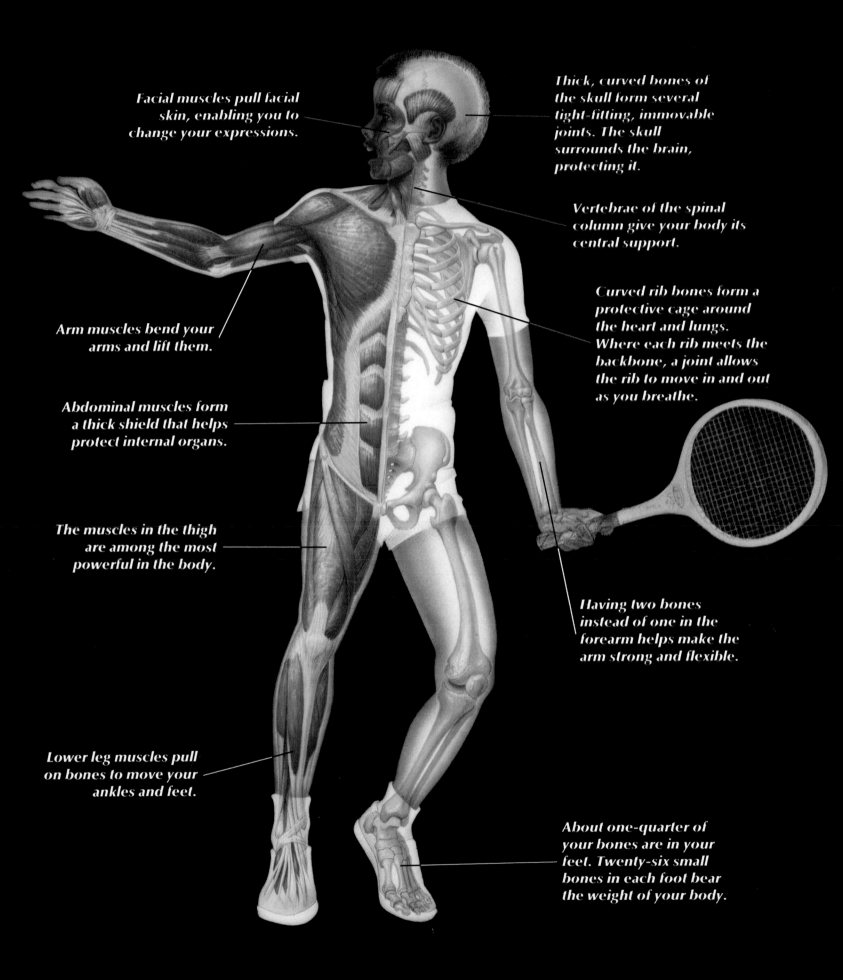

Facial muscles pull facial skin, enabling you to change your expressions.

Thick, curved bones of the skull form several tight-fitting, immovable joints. The skull surrounds the brain, protecting it.

Vertebrae of the spinal column give your body its central support.

Curved rib bones form a protective cage around the heart and lungs. Where each rib meets the backbone, a joint allows the rib to move in and out as you breathe.

Arm muscles bend your arms and lift them.

Abdominal muscles form a thick shield that helps protect internal organs.

The muscles in the thigh are among the most powerful in the body.

Having two bones instead of one in the forearm helps make the arm strong and flexible.

Lower leg muscles pull on bones to move your ankles and feet.

About one-quarter of your bones are in your feet. Twenty-six small bones in each foot bear the weight of your body.

minerals slowly began turning the cartilage into bone. Bone growth starts about seven months before birth. It continues until you are about 18 years old.

The hard outer layer of your bones is made mostly of calcium. This mineral helps make your bones strong. The outer layer is called compact bone. It appears solid, but it contains many tiny canals. They hold blood vessels and nerves. The inner layer consists of a spongy network of tissue. In fact, the layer is called spongy bone. It looks somewhat like a honeycomb. A soft material called marrow fills the spaces. Marrow supplies the material that forms blood cells.

Spongy bone forms the greatest part of a bone. Its light weight helps your muscles to move your arms, legs, and other body parts with ease.

How does a broken bone mend itself?

The mending process begins immediately. Broken blood vessels inside the bone release blood into the fracture. In about seven hours, clotted blood forms a protective substance. It helps speed the production of new bone cells. In two days, a layer of stiff tissue forms around the fracture, or break. It acts as a natural splint, holding the bone sections in place. While bone cells at the broken edges are building toward each other, blood vessels are forming a new network in the fracture.

Children's bones heal more quickly than those of adults. A fracture in a small child may heal in three weeks. The same fracture in an older person might take four months to heal.

The spinal column (right) consists of many ring-shaped vertebrae. The spinal cord passes down through the center of the spinal column. A computer has added color to this X-ray view.

A thighbone (below), sawed in half lengthwise, shows how most bones are constructed. The thin, strong outer layer is called compact bone. The inner part is called spongy bone. The spaces between ridges of bone tissue make bones light in weight.

WILLIAM S. JOBE

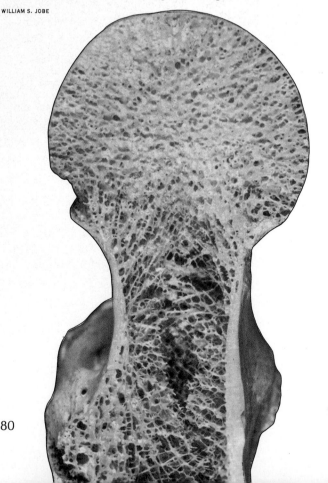

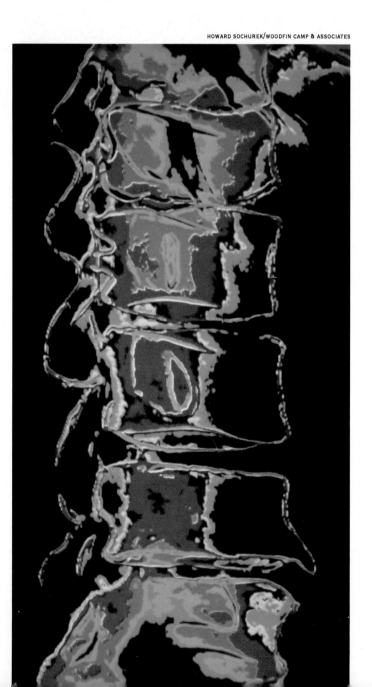

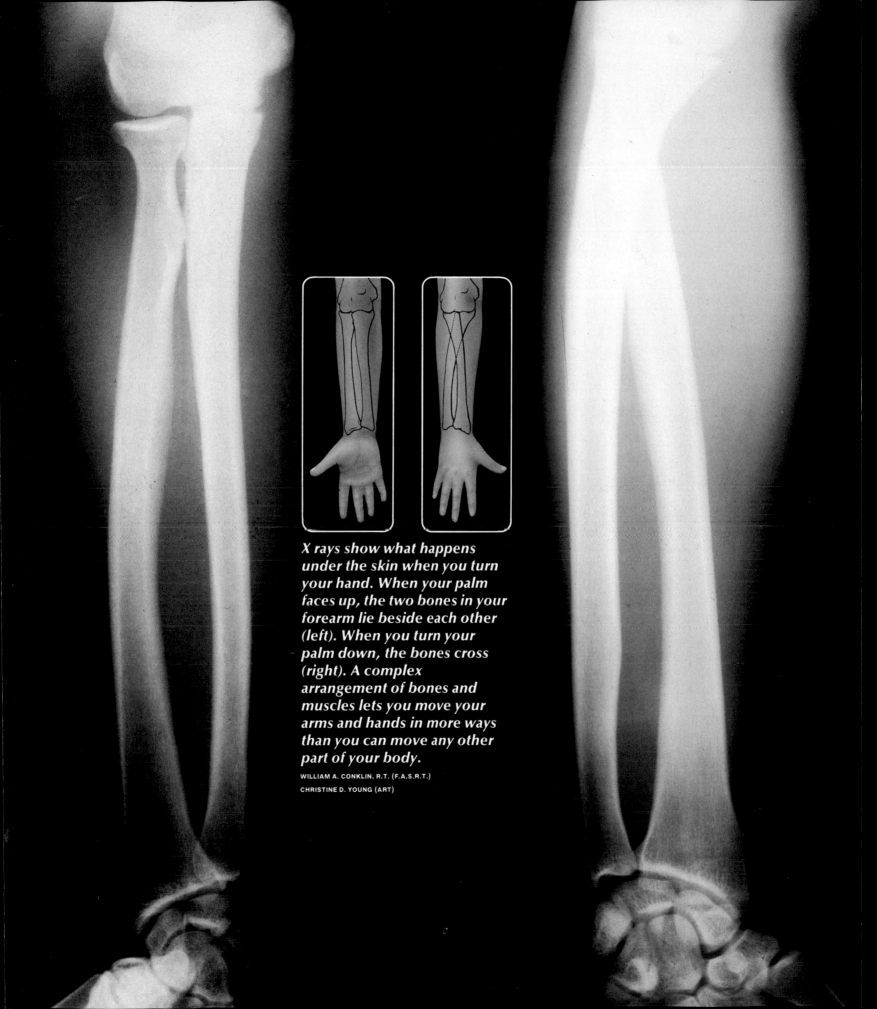

X rays show what happens under the skin when you turn your hand. When your palm faces up, the two bones in your forearm lie beside each other (left). When you turn your palm down, the bones cross (right). A complex arrangement of bones and muscles lets you move your arms and hands in more ways than you can move any other part of your body.

WILLIAM A. CONKLIN, R.T. (F.A.S.R.T.)

CHRISTINE D. YOUNG (ART)

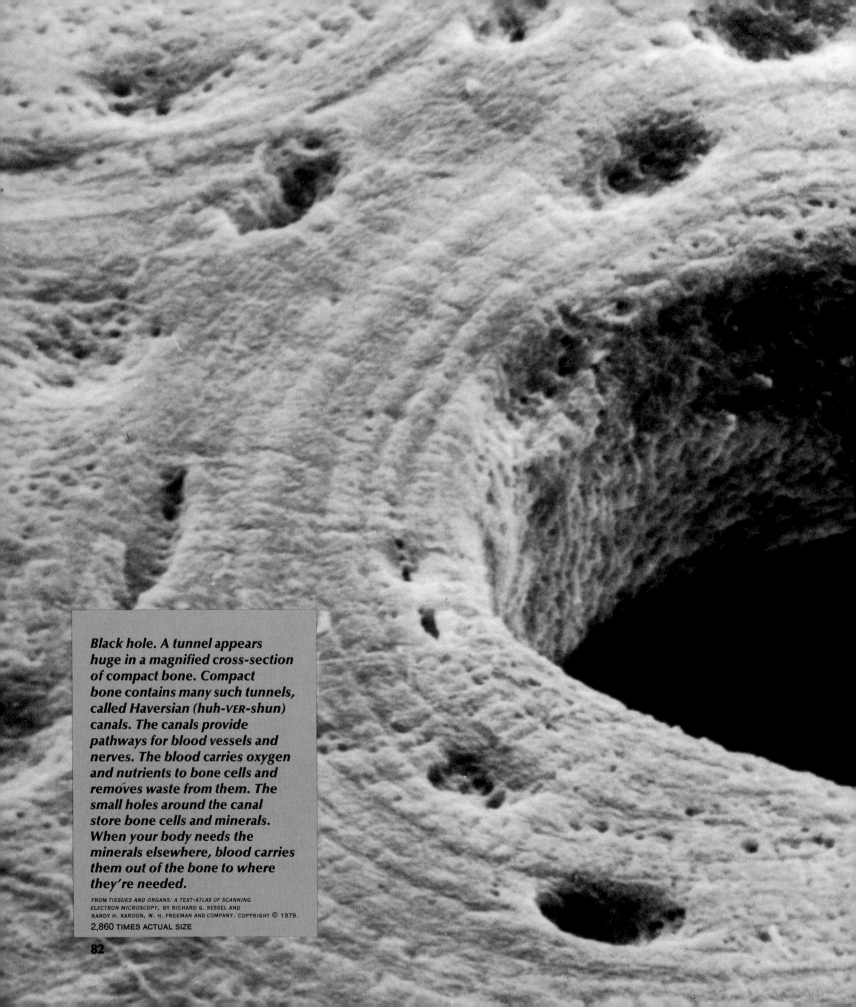

Black hole. A tunnel appears huge in a magnified cross-section of compact bone. Compact bone contains many such tunnels, called Haversian (huh-VER-shun) canals. The canals provide pathways for blood vessels and nerves. The blood carries oxygen and nutrients to bone cells and removes waste from them. The small holes around the canal store bone cells and minerals. When your body needs the minerals elsewhere, blood carries them out of the bone to where they're needed.

FROM *TISSUES AND ORGANS: A TEXT-ATLAS OF SCANNING ELECTRON MICROSCOPY*, BY RICHARD G. KESSEL AND RANDY H. KARDON, W. H. FREEMAN AND COMPANY. COPYRIGHT © 1979.

2,860 TIMES ACTUAL SIZE

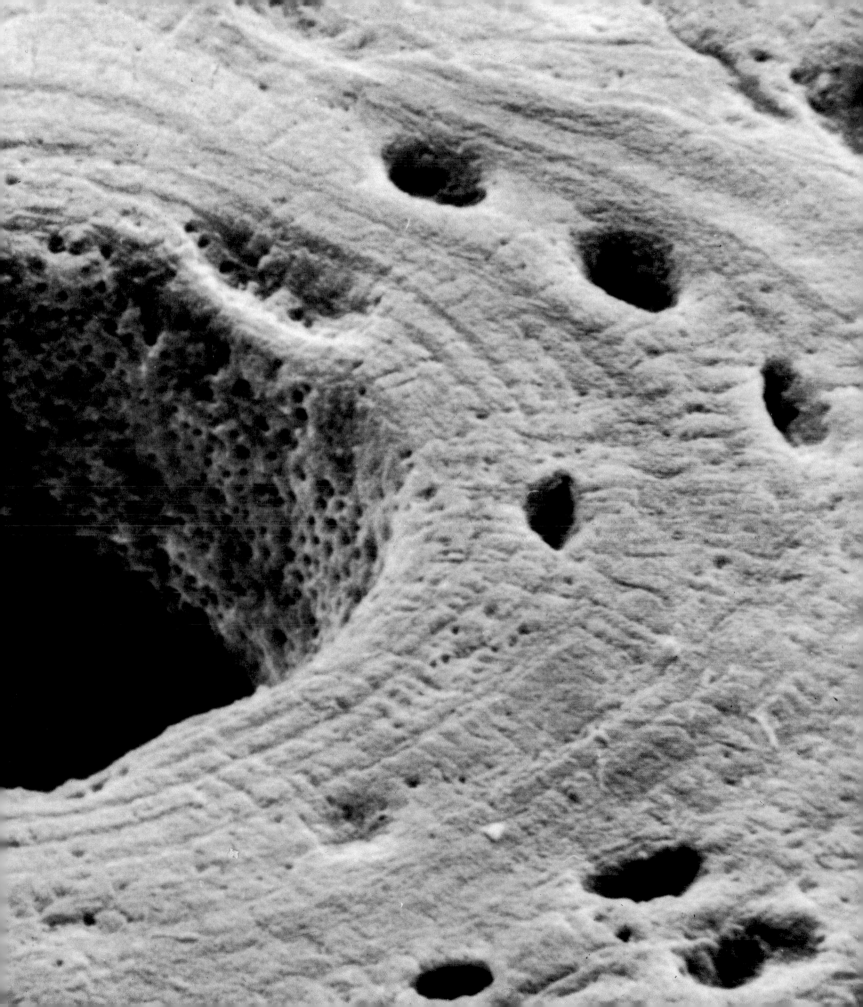

A variety of joints

Joints, where bones meet, determine the directions in which bones can move. You see several kinds of joints below. Most kinds occur in more than one part of the body.

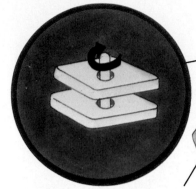

A *pivot joint* enables your head to turn from side to side. This movement allows you to take in broad scenes without turning your entire body.

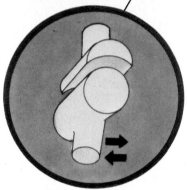

Hinge joints let your arms stretch and bend. This motion makes it possible for you to reach out to an object, to pull it, and to lift it.

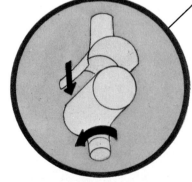

Condylar joints let your knees bend, extend, and rotate slightly. This action allows you to sit down, to stand up, and to walk smoothly.

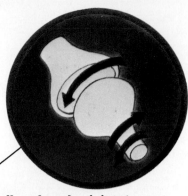

Ball-and-socket joints in your shoulders provide movement in nearly all directions. No other kind of joint lets you move in so many ways.

Ellipsoid joints let your wrists pivot up and down and sideways. They aid your hands in doing a variety of jobs.

Plane joints enable bones in your feet and toes to slide forward, backward, and sideways. They help your feet balance your body.

Saddle joints allow you to lean forward and backward at the ankles. In your thumbs, saddle joints give you a tight grip on small objects.

ROZ SCHANZER. ADAPTED FROM *ATLAS OF THE BODY AND MIND*, © MITCHELL BEAZLEY PUBLISHERS, LTD., 1976. PUBLISHED IN THE UNITED STATES BY RAND McNALLY AND CO.

How do my joints work?

Try to turn the pages of this book without bending your fingers. Try walking without bending your knees. Hard, isn't it? Joints solve such movement problems for you.

Joints occur where bones meet. Your body has many kinds of joints. Some move freely. Some move only slightly. Some, such as those in the skull, do not move at all. In movable joints, ligaments hold the ends of the bones together. Ligaments help prevent bones from slipping out of place.

The hinge joint is one kind of movable joint. The joints in your fingers are hinge joints. They work like door hinges, letting your fingers bend and extend.

Turn your head from side to side. You're using a pivot joint. It lets bones twist around. Your elbow is both a hinge joint and a pivot joint.

You can swing your arm in any direction. That's because the end of your upper-arm bone is ball-shaped. It fits into a socket in your shoulder bone. Of all the joints in your body, the ball-and-socket joint allows the greatest freedom of movement.

Your joints are protected from wear and tear in several ways. Glassy-smooth cartilage caps the ends of bones at moving joints. It allows bones to slide easily against each other. It also softens the force when bone bumps bone, as happens when you run. A thick fluid produced in the joints keeps them well lubricated. It lets the bones move like the parts of a smooth-running engine.

Skeletal muscles—those you use consciously—usually work in pairs (right, top). They pull on bones to produce motion. When the biceps (A) in your upper arm contracts, it pulls your forearm upward. The triceps (B), behind the biceps, relaxes. To lower your arm, the triceps contracts and the biceps relaxes. Ropelike tissues called tendons tie one end of these muscles to bones in your lower arms. Tendons tie the other end of the muscles to bones at the shoulder.

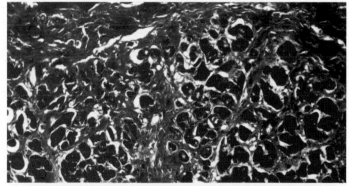

Magnified cross-section of skeletal muscle reveals red fibers (right, center). Connective tissue, in blue, binds the fibers. The photographer added the color to this slice of tissue.

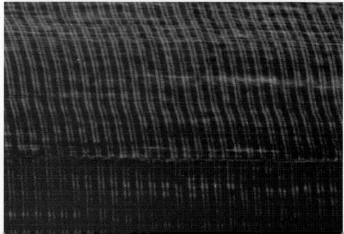

In a lengthwise section, skeletal-muscle fibers appear striped (right, bottom). The fibers lie next to each other in rows. Bundles of these fibers form skeletal muscles. Some muscles contain thousands of cells. The cells change nutrients into energy and store it. Release of this energy is triggered by a signal from the brain or the spinal column. It results in a muscle contraction.

Padded for safety, football players do stretching exercises to limber up their muscles before a game.

How can I take care of my muscles?

Playing sports or following a program of regular exercise will help strengthen your muscles. These tips from physical-fitness experts will help you go about conditioning your muscles in the right way.

● **_Train, but don't overtrain._** You can push your body too far. Training too much doesn't improve performance—and can actually hurt it. If you feel stiffness in a joint or a burning feeling in an arm or a leg, stop. You have pushed yourself too hard. Help your body by taking a rest. Resting gives muscles time to recover.

● **_Stretch._** Stretching before you play a sport gives your muscles warning. It lets them get ready to go to work running, skiing, swimming, or doing whatever other energetic activity you plan. Stretching helps prevent problems such as muscle strain and muscle ache. It helps reduce muscle tension and relax your body.

● **_Warm up._** Warming up should follow stretching. It is more vigorous. In warming up, you go through some of the motions of the activity you are about to undertake. Start out at an easy pace. Then gradually step up the pace. Warming up increases the supply of blood to the muscles. It also continues to prepare the muscles for the activity to follow.

● **_Use the right equipment._** In many sports, it is important to wear protective gear. Each of these sports has its own safety equipment. Be sure the equipment fits properly. Keep it in good condition.

A gymnast performs on a balance beam. Andrea Whitson, 11, of Silver Spring, Maryland, depends on strong bones and muscles to perform the difficult routines. Muscles tugging on bones lift, lower, bend,

88

and straighten her limbs. Such agility comes from a healthy body trained to move in response to the commands of the brain. A photographer used special lights and other equipment to capture this action on film.

7

on GUARD:
the body's defenses

John Barnett, 12, of College Park, Maryland, at left, fences with Rusty Scott, 15, of Takoma Park, Maryland. During exercise like this, the body can quickly overheat. When that happens, sweat glands start producing a fluid. The fluid evaporates on the skin, cooling the body. Below, Bod Squad members climb through sweat pores at the surface of the skin. Sweating is just one of many defenses your body can call on when the need arises.

You may not know it, but your body is constantly under attack. The enemies are microscopic invaders. You call them germs or microbes. Microbes, such as bacteria and viruses, are all around you. They live in the air you breathe, on the surface of your skin, and even in the food you eat.

Are all germs harmful?

No. Some germs actually aid certain bodily functions—digestion, for one. But some germs can make you very sick. When you get an infection or a disease, it is usually because harmful germs have invaded your body and multiplied. They attack and damage your cells.

Germs spread fast. A single bacterium can multiply into several thousand in just a few hours. If your body had no way of stopping harmful bacteria and other microbes, they would soon overwhelm you. You could not survive for very long.

Luckily, your body has defenses against these invaders. Your skin is your first line of defense.

How does my skin protect me against germs?

Skin is made up of two main layers. They are the inner layer, called the dermis, and the outer layer, called the epidermis. The cells at the surface of the epidermis form a tough, waterproof shield. Most germs can't penetrate it.

In addition, organs in the skin help control the number of germs at the surface. The dermis

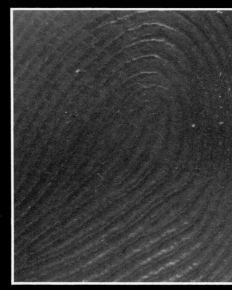

Curling ridges cover the skin at the tip of the thumb. Your fingertips also have ridges. The ridges aid in the sense of touch and help you get a firm grip on objects.

contains thousands of oil glands. The fluid they produce reaches the surface of the skin through pores. Chemicals in the oil help keep germs from multiplying.

How do germs get into my body, and what happens when they do?

Germs can invade through a cut in the skin or through any natural opening of the body. When germs invade, white blood cells arrive to attack them. There are different kinds of white blood cells, with different jobs to do. Two kinds of white blood cells have the job of defending the body against invaders. These cells are called lymphocytes (LIM-fuh-sites) and phagocytes (FAG-uh-sites). They work together to combat disease-causing germs.

Lymphocytes are the chemical-warfare branch of your body's defenses. These cells produce antibodies, chemicals that help combat germs. Antibodies travel through your bloodstream to search out invading germs. They lock onto the germs, giving them a chemical coating that identifies them as harmful. Lymphocytes manufacture thousands of kinds of antibodies. There is a different antibody for each kind of germ.

Antibodies give you immunity—the ability to resist infection and disease. Once you have had certain illnesses, such as chicken pox or the measles, you probably will never have them again. If the same kind of disease-causing germs invade another time, the lymphocytes will "remember" them and quickly produce antibodies.

Vaccines can give you *(Continued on page 95)*

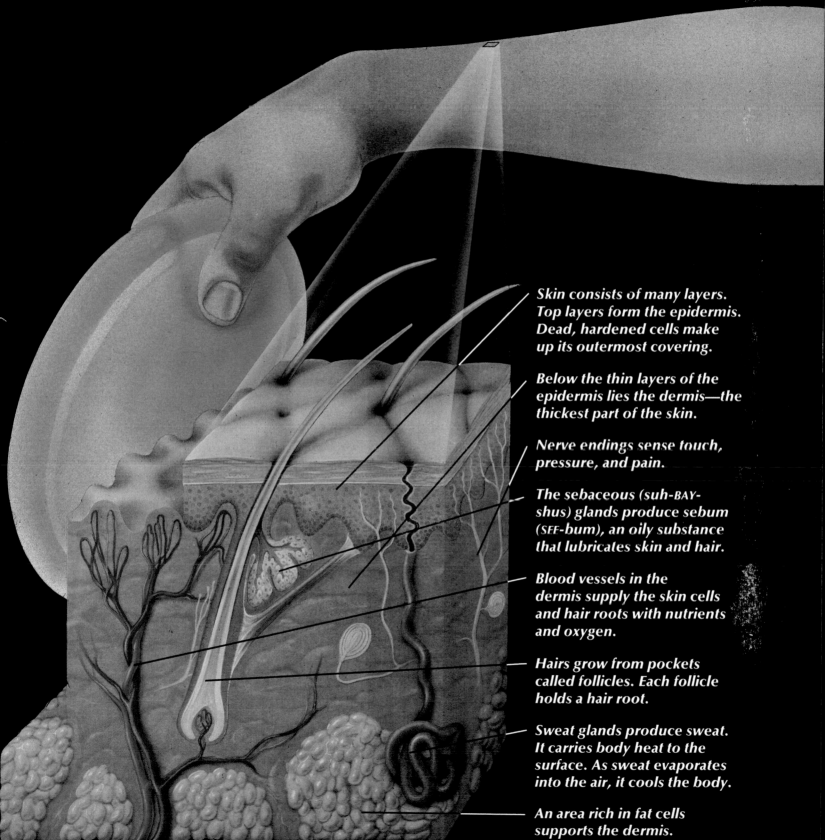

Skin consists of many layers. Top layers form the epidermis. Dead, hardened cells make up its outermost covering.

Below the thin layers of the epidermis lies the dermis—the thickest part of the skin.

Nerve endings sense touch, pressure, and pain.

The sebaceous (suh-BAY-shus) glands produce sebum (SEE-bum), an oily substance that lubricates skin and hair.

Blood vessels in the dermis supply the skin cells and hair roots with nutrients and oxygen.

Hairs grow from pockets called follicles. Each follicle holds a hair root.

Sweat glands produce sweat. It carries body heat to the surface. As sweat evaporates into the air, it cools the body.

An area rich in fat cells supports the dermis.

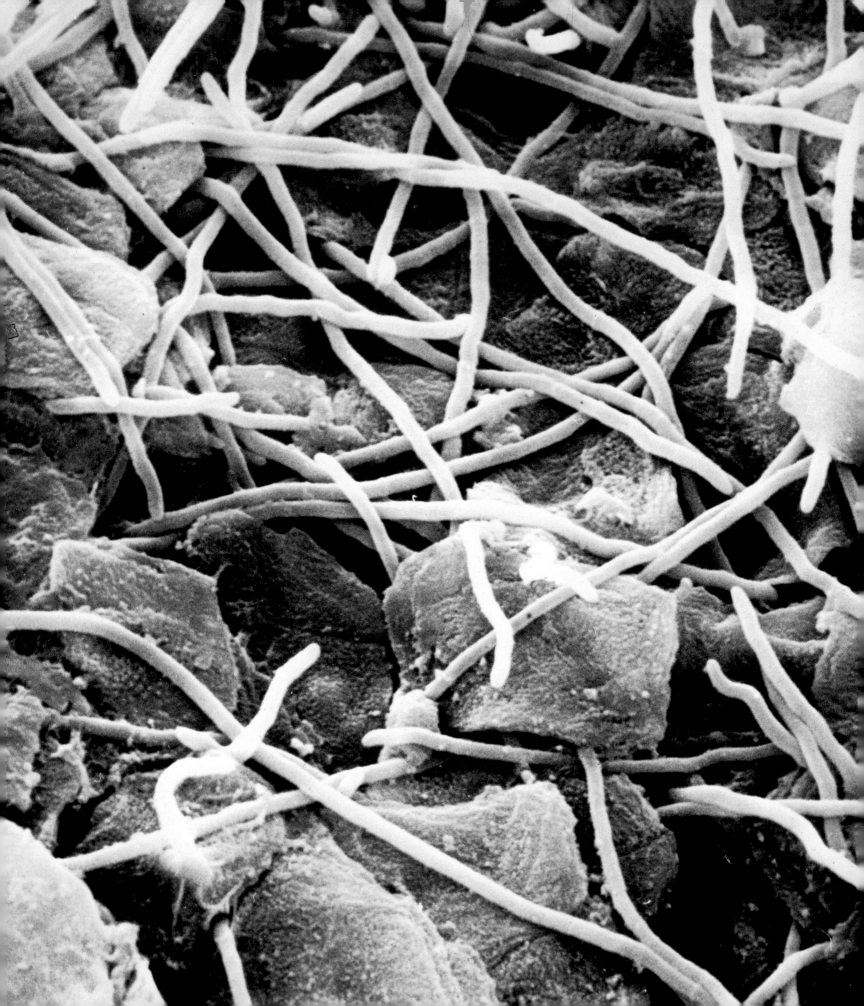

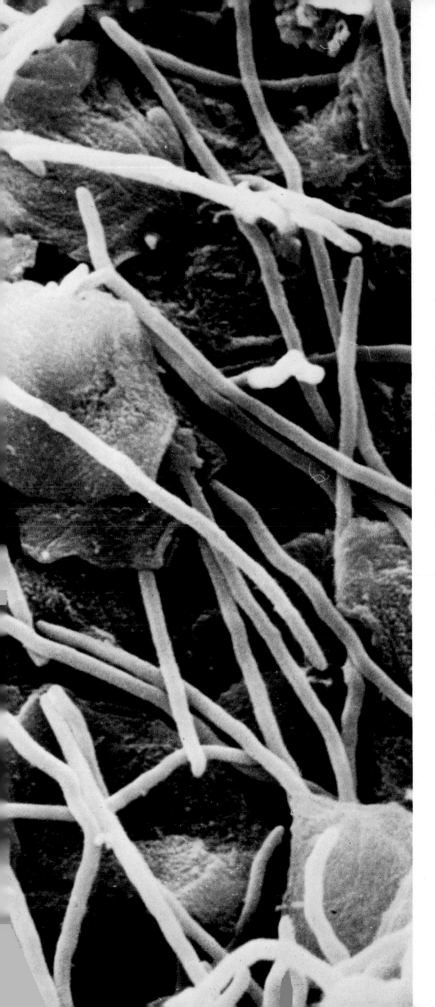

Magnified thousands of times, rod-shaped fungus cells cover a portion of skin. They are one of many kinds of microbes, or germs, that can invade your body and cause infection. Fortunately, harmful microbes like these seldom penetrate far into the body.

Cell wars! As foreign substances enter your body, white blood cells rush to destroy them. Below, a white blood cell starts to digest two invading cells.

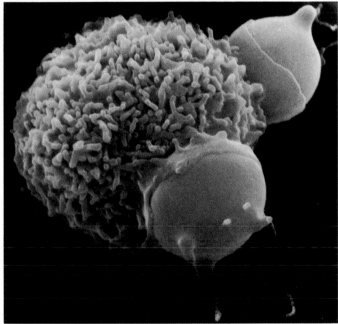

REVEL, RABINOVITCH, DE STEPHANO/CALTEC   10,000 TIMES ACTUAL SIZE

(*Continued from page 92*) immunity against some diseases, such as polio and smallpox. A vaccine is a preparation of dead or weakened germs. A vaccine doesn't give you the disease the germs usually produce, but it triggers the production of antibodies, as if you actually were ill. Vaccines can save your life by helping your body protect you.

Phagocytes, the other germ-fighting white blood cells, are the foot soldiers of the body's defense system. They surround germs and digest them with powerful enzymes. They are able to recognize harmful germs because of the chemical coating the antibodies have given them. Phagocytes are bigger than most germs. One of them can destroy large numbers of the invaders.

Some phagocytes die defending the body. The dead cells, along with body fluids, damaged tissue, and dead germs, form pus. When you see pus around a wound, you know that phagocytes have been fighting—and dying—to protect you.

3,494 TIMES ACTUAL SIZE   BIOPHOTO ASSOCIATES

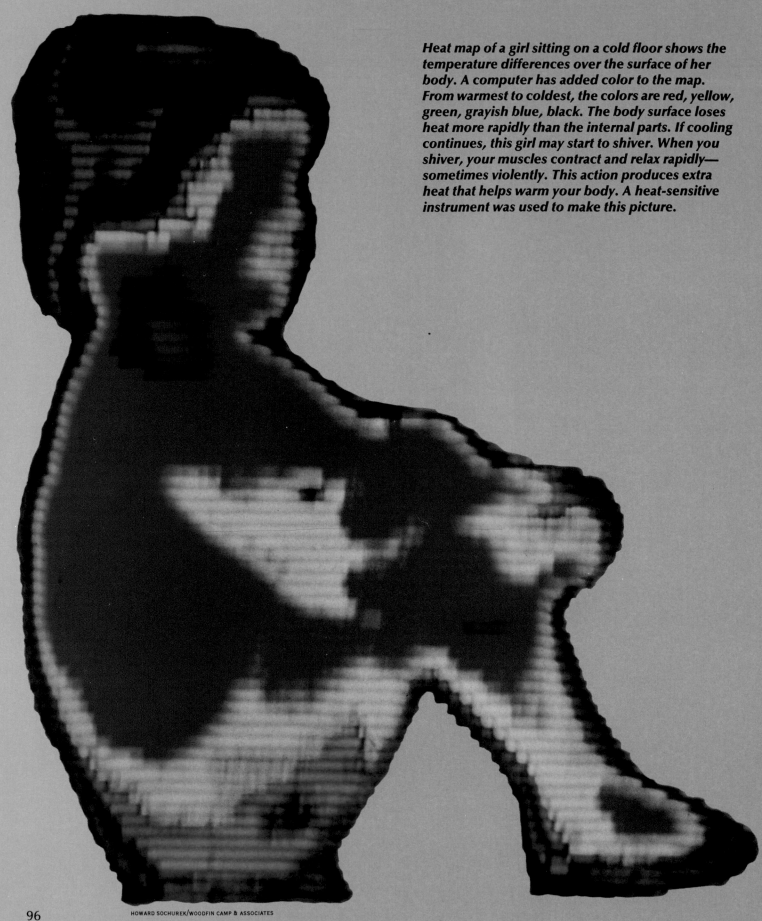

Heat map of a girl sitting on a cold floor shows the temperature differences over the surface of her body. A computer has added color to the map. From warmest to coldest, the colors are red, yellow, green, grayish blue, black. The body surface loses heat more rapidly than the internal parts. If cooling continues, this girl may start to shiver. When you shiver, your muscles contract and relax rapidly— sometimes violently. This action produces extra heat that helps warm your body. A heat-sensitive instrument was used to make this picture.

After staying outside too long on a cold winter day, Tony Brandenburg, 12, of Worthington, Minnesota, has frostbite on his cheeks (above). Frostbite occurs when water in skin tissues freezes. It makes the skin turn white and numb. Frostbite should be treated quickly by applying warm water.

She tans; he burns (top). That's because she's using an umbrella and a lotion containing a sunscreen. He is exposing his untanned skin to the midday sun. In sunlight, certain skin cells produce a dark substance called melanin

(A—above, left). Melanin absorbs ultraviolet rays. It also produces a tan. But tanning takes several days. Unprotected by melanin, vessels in the boy's skin (B—above, right) swell and fill with blood. His skin turns red and becomes painful.

Why do I get a fever when I'm sick?

When you catch some illnesses your body temperature rises, giving you a fever. The fever helps your body fight the illness. The higher temperature makes it harder for some illness-causing germs to multiply inside you.

When you are healthy, your body maintains an even temperature of about 98.6°F (37.0°C). Your organs work best at this temperature. On a cold day, blood vessels near the surface of the skin contract. That reduces the flow of blood to the cool surface, where blood loses some of its heat.

On a hot day, the blood vessels open wide to increase the flow of blood to the surface. At the same time, sweat on the skin evaporates, cooling the skin and the blood that flows through it.

Why do some people tan while others burn?

Whether you tan or burn depends on whether you are naturally fair skinned or dark skinned. It also depends on when and how long you are in the sun. The diagrams above show what happens when you tan and when you burn. Tanning is your body's way of protecting you from the sun. Your skin has cells that produce a dark, protective substance called melanin. Exposure to strong sunlight makes the cells produce an increased amount of melanin. The cells of fair-skinned people produce less melanin than the cells of dark-skinned people. The melanin absorbs ultraviolet rays, which cause burn. It also makes you turn darker. But it takes several days for your skin to produce enough melanin for a protective tan. Too much sun too quickly can give you a painful burn.

97

TERRY DOMICO/WEST STOCK

Hair grows thickly on the head, as this close-up photograph shows. You have about 100,000 hairs on your head. Each one grows about one-half inch a month (1 cm). A hair lives for about four years, falls out, and is replaced by a new one.

Straight, curly, or wavy? You inherit the type of hair you have from your ancestors. Most Orientals and North American Indians have straight hair. Most black people have very curly hair. Many people of European descent have wavy hair.

ROZ SCHANZER

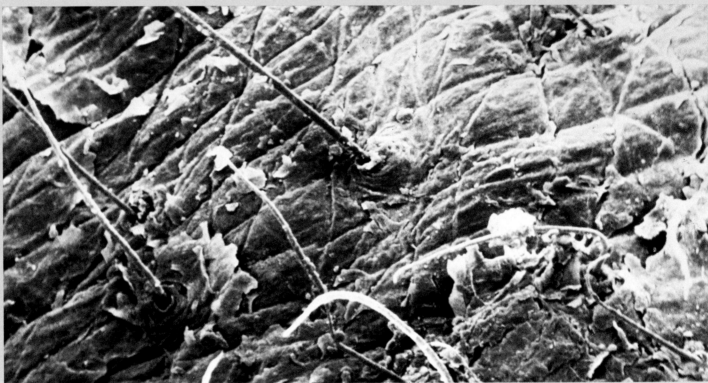

169 TIMES ACTUAL SIZE   FROM *SMALL WORLDS CLOSE UP*, BY LISA GRILLONE AND JOSEPH GENNARO, CROWN PUBLISHERS, INC. © 1978.

Under a microscope, the fine hairs that grow from your skin look like steel rods. Hair generally grows on all the surfaces of the body. Exceptions are the palms of the hands, the soles of the feet, and the lips.

Do my hair and nails serve any purpose?

Many scientists believe that hair and nails may have had important protective functions for your ancient ancestors. Today, these tissues are less important for protection than for appearance. Still, hair and nails do serve some purposes.

Eyebrows and eyelashes help shield the eyes. Hairs inside the nose and ears trap dust particles. Hair helps protect the scalp from harmful sun rays. In winter, it helps prevent the loss of body heat through the scalp.

Nails help protect the tips of your fingers and toes. Fingernails serve as tools. They help you peel fruit, pick up small objects, and scrape away such things as dried mud and dried paint drippings.

A person's hair color depends on the amount of pigment the hair contains (left). Pigment, a coloring substance, is deposited into each hair at its root. A brown hair, left, has more pigment than a blond hair. As people grow older, pigment production slows or stops. Their hair turns gray or white.

1,875 TIMES ACTUAL SIZE
BIOPHOTO ASSOCIATES

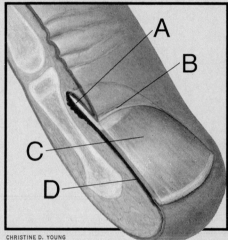

CHRISTINE D. YOUNG

Handy tools. Your fingernails help you peel an orange, pry open a paper clip, or pluck a large splinter from your skin. They also protect the sensitive tips of your fingers. A nail (above) grows from a root (A). A piece of skin (B) called the cuticle (CUTE-uh-kul) covers the root. The hard outer part of your nail, the nail plate (C), pushes outward along the nail bed (D) as new tissue forms near the root. The nail plate actually consists of dead tissue— as does hair outside the scalp. That's why you feel no pain when you trim your nails or have your hair cut.

All systems go! It takes a strong body with all its parts working together to compete in a bicycle motocross race. This boy's brain helps him steer, keep his balance, and plan racing strategy. Muscles in the boy's legs provide the pedaling power to speed him along. His sense of touch and his quick reflexes help him handle the bumps and obstacles on the track.

KEITH H. MURAKAMI/TOM STACK & ASSOCIATES

Take care—it's your body!

In this book, you've seen how your wonderful body works to keep you healthy, active, and growing. You've learned that your brain is more complex than any computer ever could be. You've seen how the body repairs itself and how it protects you from enemies too small to see. You can help your body function at its best by giving it the proper care.

Here are some things you can do to help it:

● Eat a balanced diet of nutritious foods each day. The food you eat provides building materials your body needs. Food supplies you with energy and helps you grow strong.

● Exercise regularly. Exercise helps keep your body fit by strengthening your muscles. It also improves the delivery of nutrients and oxygen to your cells.

● Get plenty of sleep. Sleep restores your energy after a day of hard work or hard play. It gives damaged cells time to repair themselves.

● Keep your skin, hair, and teeth clean. This helps prevent the growth of disease-causing germs. There's another reason for brushing and scrubbing: Good grooming actually makes you *feel* better, as well as look better.

● Finally, to be sure you stay in top condition, have regular medical and dental checkups. During such a checkup, a doctor or a dentist can detect small problems and correct them while they're still small.

Being healthy helps you enjoy life. So take care of your body—and it will take care of you.

Index

Up and over. In a town near Paris, France, two playmates romp in a game of leapfrog. Exercise such as this helps keep the body strong and healthy. Rest and a well-balanced diet also help.

G. MARCHE/FREELANCE PHOTOGRAPHERS GUILD

ADDITIONAL READING

Readers may want to check the *National Geographic Index* in a school or a public library for related articles and to refer to the following books. ("A" indicates a book for readers at the adult level.)

The cell and growth: Pfeiffer, John, *The Cell,* Time Inc., 1964 (A). Tanner, James M., et al., *Growth,* Time Inc., 1965 (A).

The nervous system: Fincher, Jack, *The Brain,* U. S. News Books, 1981 (A). Kalina, Sigmund, *Your Nerves and Their Messages,* Lothrop, Lee and Shepard, 1973. National Geographic Society, *Frontiers of Science,* 1982 (A). Restak, Richard M., *The Brain: The Last Frontier,* 1979, Doubleday (A). Silverstein, Alvin, and Virginia Silverstein, *Exploring The Brain,* Prentice-Hall, 1973. Silverstein, Alvin, and Virginia Silverstein, *The Nervous System: The Inner Networks,* Prentice-Hall, 1971. Silverstein, Alvin, and Virginia Silverstein, *Sleep and Dreams,* J. B. Lippincott, 1974. Weart, Edith L., *The Story of Your Brain and Nerves,* Coward-McCann, 1961.

The respiratory system: Simon, Seymour, *About Your Lungs,* McGraw-Hill, 1978. Ward, Brian, *The Lungs and Breathing,* Warwick Press, 1981.

The digestive system: Bershad, Carol, and Deborah Bernick, *Bodyworks: The Kids' Guide to Food and Physical Fitness,* Random House, 1979. Burns, Marilyn, *Good For Me! All About Food in 32 Bites,* Little, Brown, 1978. Elgin, Kathleen, *The Human Body: The Digestive System,*

Franklin Watts, 1973. Nourse, Alan, *The Tooth Book,* David McKay, 1977. U. S. Department of Agriculture, *What's To Eat?,* Government Printing Office, 1979. Zim, Herbert S., *Your Stomach and Digestive Tract,* William Morrow, 1973.

The circulatory system: Riedman, Sarah R., *Your Blood and You,* Abelard-Schuman, 1963. Weart, Edith L., *The Story of Your Blood,* Coward, McCann and Geoghegan, 1960. Zim, Herbert S., *Blood,* William Morrow, 1970.

The skeletal system: Allen, Gwen, *Bones,* Franklin Watts, 1970. Gallant, Roy, *Me and My Bones,* Doubleday, 1971. Zim, Herbert S., *Bones,* William Morrow, 1969.

The body's defenses: Doss, Helen, *Your Skin Holds You In,* Julian Messner, 1978. Knight, David C., *Your Body's Defenses,* McGraw-Hill, 1975. Zim, Herbert S., *Your Skin,* William Morrow, 1979.

Exercise: Cosgrove, Margaret, *Your Muscles and Ways to Exercise Them,* Dodd, Mead, 1980. Mirkin, Gabe, and Marshall Hoffman, *The Sportsmedicine Book,* Little, Brown, 1978 (A). Schneider, Tom, *Everybody's a Winner,* Little, Brown, 1976. Southmayd, William, and Marshall Hoffman, *Sports Health: The Complete Book of Athletic Injuries,* Quick Fox, 1981 (A).

CONSULTANTS

Robert H. Parrott, M.D., Director, Children's Hospital National Medical Center, and Chairman, Department of Child Health and Development, George Washington University; Richard B. Reff, M.D., Assistant Professor of Orthopedic Surgery, Department of Child Health and Development, George Washington University, and pediatric orthopedic surgeon, Children's Hospital National Medical Center—*Chief Consultants*

Glenn O. Blough, LL.D., University of Maryland; Patricia Leadbetter King, National Cathedral School; Violet A. Tibbetts—*Educational Consultants*

Nicholas J. Long, Ph.D.—*Consulting Psychologist*

The Special Publications and School Services Division is grateful to the individuals named or quoted within the text and to those cited here for their generous assistance:

Margaret Abernathy, M.D., Georgetown University School of Medicine; Jennifer Bell, M.D., Columbia–Presbyterian Medical Center; William C. Black, M.D., Hackensack Hospital; Anthony J. Caputy, M.D., Georgetown University Medical Center; Robert L. Carter, M.D., McLean, Virginia; Richard Cendali, Boulder, Colorado; Thomas M. Crisp, Ph.D., Georgetown University School of Medicine.

Alan I. Fields, M.D., Children's Hospital National Medical Center; William H. Frey II, Ph.D., St. Paul–Ramsey Medical Center; Frank M. Galioto, Jr., M.D., Children's Hospital National Medical Center; Robert I. Henkin, M.D., Georgetown University Medical Center; Judith M. Hobart; Joseph Irr, Ph.D., E. I. du Pont de Nemours & Company; Richard O. Keelor, Ph.D., President's Council on Physical Fitness and Sports.

Kunio Mizuta, Embassy of Japan; Corinne M. Montandon, Dr. P.H., R.D., Baylor College of Medicine; Richard M. Restak, M.D., Georgetown University School of Medicine; Moses S. Schanfield, Ph.D., and Susan Schoeppner, American Red Cross; Anthony J. Sciuto, D.M.D., Haverhill, Massachusetts; Faustino Suarez, M.D., Georgetown University School of Medicine; Jane L. Todaro, M.D., Children's Hospital National Medical Center; Mark W. Townsend, Environmental Protection Agency.

Composition for YOUR WONDERFUL BODY! by National Geographic's Photographic Services, Carl M. Shrader, Director; Lawrence F. Ludwig, Assistant Director. Printed and bound by Holladay-Tyler Printing Corp., Rockville, Md. Color separations by the Lanman-Progressive Co., Washington, D. C.; Lincoln Graphics, Inc., Cherry Hill, N.J.; NEC, Inc., Nashville, Tenn. FAR-OUT FUN! printed by Federated Lithographers and Printers, Inc., Providence, R.I.; *Classroom Activities Folder* produced by Mazer Corp., Dayton, Ohio.

Library of Congress CIP Data
Main entry under title:
Your wonderful body!
  (Books for world explorers)
  Bibliography: p.
  Includes index.
  SUMMARY: Discusses the functions of the human body in a question-and-answer format, emphasizing ways of keeping the body fit and healthy. Includes a wall poster, games, and puzzles.
    1. Body, Human—Juvenile literature. [1. Body, Human. 2. Questions and answers] I. National Geographic Society (U. S.) II. Series.
QP37.Y67   1982   612   81-47892
ISBN 0-87044-423-9 (regular binding)
ISBN 0-87044-428-X (library binding)

PUBLISHED BY
THE NATIONAL GEOGRAPHIC SOCIETY
WASHINGTON, D. C.

Gilbert M. Grosvenor, *President*
Melvin M. Payne, *Chairman of the Board*
Owen R. Anderson, *Executive Vice President*
Robert L. Breeden, *Vice President,
Publications and Educational Media*

PREPARED BY THE SPECIAL PUBLICATIONS
AND SCHOOL SERVICES DIVISION

Donald J. Crump, *Director*
Philip B. Silcott, *Associate Director*
William L. Allen, William R. Gray, *Assistant Directors*

STAFF FOR BOOKS FOR WORLD EXPLORERS
Ralph Gray, *Editor*
Pat Robbins, *Managing Editor*
Ursula Perrin Vosseler, *Art Director*

STAFF FOR *YOUR WONDERFUL BODY!*
  Ross Bankson, *Managing Editor*
  Alison Wilbur Eskildsen, *Picture Editor*
  Viviane Y. Silverman, *Designer*
  Richard M. Crum, *Contributing Editor*
  Robin Darcey Dennis (chapters 1, 2, 6), Catherine O'Neill (chapters 3, 4, 5), Judith E. Rinard ("Go for It!", chapter 7), *Writers*
  Mary B. Campbell, Mary Lee Elden, *Researchers*
  Mary Elizabeth Davis, *Editorial Assistant*
  Artemis S. Lampathakis, *Illustrations Assistant*
  Mary Jane Gore, *Art Secretary*

STAFF FOR *FAR-OUT FUN!* Patricia N. Holland, *Project Editor;* Roger B. Hirschland, *Text Editor;* Beth Molloy, *Designer;* Dru Colbert, *Artist*

ENGRAVING, PRINTING, AND PRODUCT MANUFACTURE
Robert W. Messer, *Manager;* George V. White, *Production Manager;* Mark R. Dunlevy, *Production Project Manager;* Richard A. McClure, David V. Showers, Gregory Storer, *Assistant Production Managers;* Katherine H. Donohue, *Senior Production Assistant;* Mary A. Bennett, *Production Assistant;* Katherine R. Leitch, *Production Staff Assistant*

STAFF ASSISTANTS: Nancy F. Berry, Pamela A. Black, Rebecca Bittle, Nettie Burke, Claire M. Doig, Janet A. Dustin, Rosamund Garner, Victoria D. Garrett, Jane R. Halpin, Nancy J. Harvey, Sheryl A. Hoey, Joan Hurst, Virginia A. McCoy, Mary Evelyn McKinney, Merrick P. Murdock, Cleo Petroff, Victoria I. Piscopo, Tammy Presley, Carol A. Rocheleau, Kathleen T. Shea, Katheryn M. Slocum, Jenny Takacs

MARKET RESEARCH: Mark W. Brown, Marjorie E. Hofman, Carrla L. Holmes, Meg McElligott Kieffer

INDEX: Brit Aabakken Peterson